ADVANCED
WORLDBUILDING
CHARACTERS

CREATED BY **JAIME BUCKLEY**

ADVANCED WORLDBUILDING CHARACTERS
Custom templates for creative writers

Created by Jaime Buckley
Copyright © 2018 Jaime D. Buckley. All rights reserved.

For more information about this book and other books by the author,
please visit advancedworldbuilding.com

Published by On The Fly Publications
https://OnTheFlyPublications.com

First Publishing: 2018
Printed in the USA

ISBN# 978-1-61463-097-5

Cover Design & Illustrations by Jaime Buckley

For more fictional works, visit the author at JaimeBuckley.com

Your Characters Are KEY

Yes, every story requires worldbuilding, but how much time do writers spend cultivating dynamic characters?

Characters are the heart and seasoning of every good story—and yet how many of us fail to weave the intricate lives of those we want readers to fall in love with, love to hate, or cheer on to the bitter end?

This special journal was created to help you both develop and organize the people of your worlds, so you can draw on the raw data and bring realism whenever you need it for your writing craft.

I've always found a measure of success in everything I do for three distinct reasons:

1)   Learning and developing better tools and sharing them with others, so they can achieve their own goals and dreams keeps me soft, humble and motivated;

2)   My definition of success is 'being able to do what I love to support the people I love, and spend more time with them.' That's exACTLY what I get to do each and every day as a professional illustrator and writer, and;

3)   I started selling both my books and my services the moment in accepted a simple fact: Nothing is perfect.

No matter what you do or how hard you try, your book will not be perfect. That doesn't mean we should ignore good practices, but too often writers lose out on incredible opportunities because they are fixated on getting everything 'just right'. Hence in 2004 I made the conscious decision to accept my creative process as "success in motion".

Do the best I know how with what I have and release it to the world.

Then build on it.

That's how this Character Journal came to be in your hands.

You now possess a tool to hone your creative skills, gather them in one place and then organize them for future use. Everything you need to capture and catalogue your characters is in this journal.

Best part is, when you succeed, I succeed—because your success proves that sharing ideas and resources was the right thing to do. That helping someone else was better that being selfish, critical or greedy.

So thank you for that.

Understanding the Structure of this Journal

If you are anything like me, you are not a linear creator.

That means you like to ponder, dream, craft and then record amazing things all out of order.

In that case, this journal will fit you like a glove.

If you are nothing like me and prefer to structure each and every creation from A to Z, then this journal will also fit you like a glove.

It was was crafted to utilize both the outside and the inside, taking all your world knowledge and arranging it in whatever way you prefer.

If you notice the cover, I've removed my branding from the top of the page for you to take a marker and brand it with your own title.

The spine is also blank so you can write your own title and volume number (in case you need more than one journal).

On the inside, I've done the exact same thing, giving you the option to brand this journal with your brilliance, not mine. In fact, once you understand my simple process or create your own, you can rip out these few instructional pages and make this journal your own in every way.

This was all done on purpose.

At closer examination, you will see that the order of this journal is specific.

The first thing is a list of character 'trigger questions' to give you some starting fuel for your creative process.

If you haven't read my 'Advanced Worldbuilding Guide', you may not know what a 'trigger question' is. Think of these as mental prompts that encourage your brain to be more creative without forcing yourself—or having to struggle with the dreaded writers block (see my Advanced Worldbuilding Guide for more details).

There is a table of contents, which is blank—so when you are done with your creative process, you can organize your notes into sections. You'll also notice that you have an index at the back of the journal, which allows you to list subjects and then record all the various pages where the subject can be found throughout your notes. This is so helpful to keep track of random thoughts without restricting your creative flow.

The Journal also has it's own page number boxes, so you can use whatever numbering system you prefer—or make up whatever you want.

Next, you'll find character templates. Forms to organize key information like protagonists and antagonists, allowing you to recall stats with a glance while you're writing your books. At the bottom of these templates are more 'trigger' questions to assist you in writing. Again, these are specific prompts that compel your brain to be creative without having to force yourself.

This journal has 92 character sheets for you to develop protagonists, deuteragonists, antagonists, love interests, mentors, narrators, secondary characters and even flat characters.

If you require more templates, PDF copies are available at an additional price through Advanced-Worldbuilding.com, but just so you know—after using this method over the years myself, the number of forms included have always been a sufficient number for my own projects.

More on the templates in a moment.

After your templates and trigger questions you'll find the largest section of this Journal are 'blank' pages to write down your ideas as they come to you. The pages contain faded grey lines allowing you to both write and sketch without too many distractions.

How to Use This Journal

The number one rule of using this Journal successfully is: there are no rules.

My own belief is that the creative process should not be limited or boxed in. Yes, there should be guidelines and parameters, but I've learned over the years that the most important things I could do as a writer was to record ideas as they come to me.

It doesn't matter where or when ideas come, I simply need to write down the idea and not question it.

It's amazing how many times I've written something in a Journal, thinking it was useless information or something less than stellar—only to find myself in a pickle while writing a book years later, and that seemingly obtuse fact or tid-bit of knowledge turned out to be the perfect answer to my challenge.

So the last thing I want to do here is confine you to any particular methodology.

The biggest challenge you're likely to encounter is how to use the templates.

You see symbols for male and female and bars with 'importance', 'influence' and a set of characteristics like strength, streetwise and diplomacy attached to them. My intention was to allow you to circle the gender of choice and then shade in each bar according to the trait of your character, so when you are writing your stories, you can look at your main character and be reminded of who they are at a glance.

The templates also allow you to expand your thoughts with personalities, physical descriptions, unique talents and abilities, even discerning features. To take it a step further, you'll be able to list relationships and connections, habits, mannerisms and even the internal and external conflicts your character may be going through.

In the end, you'll be able to determine what the personal arc your character has in any given story

It's all up to you.

This isn't my Journal—it's yours, and that is my point here.

These are for you to use in any way you desire and to categorize what the stats mean to you. So don't limit yourself. Think about what you want these template stats to mean and use them as you see fit.

When you're done filling out the blank pages and templates, take the time to organize your Table of Contents and Index so you can find everything you crafted with ease and efficiency.

There's More To Come

My desire is to provide tools for my fellow authors, so we can share our stories with the world.

I was asked to create this journal over and over again, so here it is.

I've also been asked to create a series of reference books so that a writer could craft a complete world encyclopedia by topic.

You now have characters, so *animals* come next.

If you have any comments, questions or requests, feel free to contact me at jaimebuckley@wantedhero.com.

Good Luck Worldbuilder!

Jaime Buckley

Trigger Questions

What is a Trigger Question?

In its most basic form, a trigger question is something that generates more questions and forces your mind to answer those questions—throwing in twists as you go.

Think of it as an expansive process of creation.

The result of using trigger questions is a trail of logic as to WHY the EVENT happened in your story and how the world around it (your CORE) would be connected to it. In short, trigger questions are a catalyst to form ideas for writing a brilliant story.

The following information was created to be used in conjunction with the book Advanced WORLDBUILDING: A unique guide & journal for every writer (version 2.0), and our new Advanced WORLDBUILDING Templates 2.0 (available exclusively through wantedhero.com). Though the questions are valuable to writers wanting to create a fictional world of exceptional depth, they are best used with the "UP-CHUCK" method (gross, I know, but you'll remember it, I promise).

Trigger questions are for those struggling for ideas and who might not know where to start.

Below are a few questions to ask yourself—prompts to ingest, to tickle your mind with possibilities.

The trick with creativity is not to force it.

Never force it.

Just enjoy the process of free-thinking and write it all down as you go—doesn't matter how silly it may be at first—all things are connected.

Trust me. Keep a separate pad nearby. Creativity should not be hindered.

By the way…notes are never perfect. They are a means to an end, which is why I like to provide templates—so you won't be slowed down, even if you make a mistake.

These questions should help you form more questions. Write them down. They'll be needed for the next stage of the UP-Chuck Method…

Character Development Trigger Questions

Ask yourself these questions when you're developing people & personalities…and if they prompt OTHER questions—make sure to WRITE THEM DOWN!!

1)	Does your character sleep with his/her closet doors open or closed?

2)	Does your character sleep with your sheets tucked in or out? Does he/she sleep with feet under covers or hanging out?

3)	Has your character stolen anything before? Gum from a store? A book from the library? A street sign or maybe a car?

4) Does your character cut out coupons but then never use them? Does your character leave tips for waitresses?

5) Would your character rather be attacked by a big bear, a swarm of bees or be chewed out by an entitled millennial?

6) Does your character have freckles?

7) Does your character always smile for pictures?

8) What is your characters biggest irritation with others?

9) Does your character ever count your steps when you walk or avoid stepping on cracks?

10) Has your character ever peed or pooped in the woods? How about peed on an electric fence?

11) Has your character ever dance even if theres no music playing?

12) Does your character chew their pens and pencils?

13) Does your character still watch cartoons?

14) Does your character drink beer or wine with dinner?

15) What is your characters favorite food?

16) Has your character ever ran out of gas?

17) How many languages can your character speak?

18) Does your character have any magazine subscriptions?

19) Is your character addicted to any popular TV shows?

20) Is your character afraid of heights?

21) Does your character sing in the car?

22) Does your character sing in the shower?

23) Does your character dance in the bathroom, or in the kitchen while cooking?

24) Does your character use a gun?

25) What is your characters favorite Holliday?

26) Does your character believe in ghosts?

27) Does your character ever have a Deja-vu feeling?

28) Does your character take vitamins daily?

29) Does your character wear slippers?

30) Does your character wear a bath robe?

31) Has your character ever cried because they were so happy?

32) Has your character ever been in love?

33) Does your character prefer hot tea or cold tea?

34) Does your character prefer tea or coffee?

35) Does your character prefer sugar cookies or snickerdoodles?

36) Can your character swim well?

37) Can your character hold your breath without holding their nose?

38) Has your character ever won a contest?

39) Has your character ever had plastic surgery?

40) Can your character knit or crochet?

41) Does your character want to get married? Why? To whom??

42) If married, how long have they been married?

43) Who was your characters high school crush?

44) Does your character cry and throw a fit until they get their own way?

45) Does your character have kids?

46) Does your character want kids?

47) Does your character miss anyone right now?

General People Questions

1) How do people feel about foreigners, especially non-humans?

2) How ready are people to accept different ideas or even different perspectives to commonly held beliefs?

3) Is it easy or hard for a person born into poverty to advance to the middle class, or for a middle class person to advance to the upper class or even nobility?

4) How much resistance would there be for someone trying to rise above their station? Would such a person ever be accepted socially?

5) What things are considered luxuries--chocolate, coffee, cotton, flush toilets, spices?

6) What do people in general look like? Would a blonde (red-head, brunette) stand out in a crowd? Someone 5' tall? 7' tall?

7) Do non-humans stand out in a crowd?

8) What is furniture like? Do people craft big and blocky, delicate, simple, elaborately carved or decorated items? What is it mostly made of--cloth (like a hammock), wood, stone, etc.?

9) Are certain things (like chairs with arms or dragon-claw feet) reserved for

high-status individuals?

10) Do things like furniture design reflect the customs of people?

11) How do common aspects of living (such as faucets, toilets, bathing) differ from city to farm?

12) How do people cope with various disasters--fire, floods, volcanoes, plague, etc.?

13) How early do people get up in the morning in the city? How about in the country?

14) Are clocks common? How do people tell the time? By the sun? By listening for church bells? Using animals, such as a rooster?

15) Are certain clothes customary for certain occupations, such as military uniforms, judges' robes, sports team uniforms, servants clothes or political positions?

16) Is it the color of the clothes or style that is most important to people?

17) Are there laws defining who can wear what? What are the penalties?

18) How many changes of clothes can a normal person afford? What about a noble person? Or a peasant?

19) What are current fashion in clothes like? (Think about the hats, jewelry, shoes, both casual and formal clothing)

20) Do such fashions differ for humans/non-humans? How about from country to country?

21) What styles are considered tacky and vulgar, and what is stylish?

22) What types of decorations and accessories are common?

23) What colors and combinations of colors are thought to look well together, or to clash?

24) Do opinions of this vary from race to race, class to class or region to region?

25) What physical types and characteristics are currently fashionable? Think about tan vs. pale skin, fat vs. thin, blonde vs. brunette, muscles vs. couch potato.

26) Do people make oaths with one another? If so, what will people swear by?

27) What do people use as curse words?

28) What are the most desired/most valuable things in your society? Why is it desired/valued? Do different races value different things?

29) What are the most controversial subjects in your new culture?

30) What subjects or actions cause embarrassment or discomfort?

31) What are the society's mores regarding courtship, marriage, and family?

32) Is marriage primarily a civil or a religious institution?

33) What are the standards of beauty for people?

34) What kind of ideal life do people aspire to?

35) What kinds of people are the rebels and outcasts of this society?

36) How does society deal with them--prison, exile, decapitation, reformation, etc?

37) Who are opposed to law?

38) Are there things it is considered rude to accept?

TABLE OF CONTENTS

CONTENT TOPIC	PAGES

TABLE OF CONTENTS

CONTENT TOPIC	PAGES

TABLE OF CONTENTS

CONTENT TOPIC	PAGES

TABLE OF CONTENTS

CONTENT TOPIC	PAGES

TABLE OF CONTENTS

CONTENT TOPIC	PAGES

TABLE OF CONTENTS

CONTENT TOPIC

PAGES

TABLE OF CONTENTS

CONTENT TOPIC   PAGES

NAME _____   BOOK _____

NICKNAME _____   Series _____

IMPORTANCE				
INFLUENCE				
STRENGTH				
COORDINATION				
INTELLIGENCE				
WISDOM				
STREETWISE				
DIPLOMACY				
CHARISMA				
WILL				

Race: _____

Age: _____ Weight: _____

PORTRAIT

LAWFUL GOOD   CHAOTIC GOOD

N

LAWFUL EVIL   CHAOTIC EVIL

OCCUPATION: _____

Roll In Story:

_____
_____
_____
_____
_____
_____
_____
_____
_____
_____

Physical Description

_____
_____
_____
_____
_____

Personality

_____
_____
_____
_____
_____
_____

Discerning Features

_____
_____
_____
_____

Unique Talents / Abilities:

_____
_____
_____
_____
_____

Character TRIGGER Questions:

- Is your character considered normal and acceptable in this society? Why not?
- Does your character have any mannerisms, habits or desires considered taboo?
- What does your character do that causes others to feel uncomfortable?
- Does he / she have any special needs that have to be met (such as medication or therapy)?
- Does your character have an unknown connection to a famous / infamous person or group in history?
- Does your character have a deep secret that could change the course of events?
- What are your characters core beliefs ? Name three (3) principles they will not compromise.

- What is the greatest loss your character has experienced?
- What is your characters greatest fear? How does that affect the way they make decisions?
- What are your characters dreams? What we desire forms our decisions, so what does he / she want?
- Does your character have any specific prejudices? What are they and how do they affect interactions with others?
- Does he / she have an overpowering addiction considered a weakness...or perhaps a strength?
- Do they have a latent ability (or repressed memory) that can be brought out in the story?
- Is your character being used as a pawn in a much bigger plot behind the scenes?
- What lie have they told that will soon catch up & expose them?

FATHER:

MOTHER:

SIBLINGS:

FRIENDS:

HABITS / MANNERISMS

INTERNAL / EXTERNAL CONFLICTS:

PERSONAL STORY ARC

CHARACTER HISTORY

NAME _____

NICKNAME _____

BOOK _____

Series _____

IMPORTANCE | | | |
INFLUENCE | | | |

STRENGTH | | | |
COORDINATION | | | |

INTELLIGENCE | | | |
WISDOM | | | |
STREETWISE | | | |
DIPLOMACY | | | |
CHARISMA | | | |
WILL | | | |

Race: _____

Age: _____ Weight: _____

PORTRAIT

LAWFUL GOOD   CHAOTIC GOOD

N

LAWFUL EVIL   CHAOTIC EVIL

OCCUPATION:

Roll In Story:

Physical Description

Personality

Discerning Features

Unique Talents / Abilities:

Character TRIGGER Questions:

-Is your character considered normal and acceptable in this society? Why not?
- Does your character have any mannerisms, habits or desires considered taboo?
- What does your character do that causes others to feel uncomfortable?
- Does he / she have any special needs that have to be met (such as medication or therapy)?
- Does your character have an unknown connection to a famous / infamous person or group in history?
- Does your character have a deep secret that could change the course of events?
- What are your characters core beliefs ? Name three (3) principles they will not compromise.

- What is the greatest loss your character has experienced?
- What is your characters greatest fear? How does that affect the way they make decisions?
- What are your characters dreams? What we desire forms our decisions, so what does he / she want?
- Does your character have any specific prejudices? What are they and how do they affect interactions with others?
- Does he / she have an overpowering addiction considered a weakness...or perhaps a strength?
- Do they have a latent ability (or repressed memory) that can be brought out in the story?
- Is your character being used as a pawn in a much bigger plot behind the scenes?
- What lie have they told that will soon catch up & expose them?

FATHER:

MOTHER:

SIBLINGS:

FRIENDS:

HABITS / MANNERISMS

INTERNAL / EXTERNAL CONFLICTS:

PERSONAL STORY ARC

CHARACTER HISTORY

NAME _____

NICKNAME _____

BOOK _____

Series _____

IMPORTANCE				
INFLUENCE				
STRENGTH				
COORDINATION				
INTELLIGENCE				
WISDOM				
STREETWISE				
DIPLOMACY				
CHARISMA				
WILL				

Race: _____

Age: _____   Weight: _____

LAWFUL GOOD   CHAOTIC GOOD

N

LAWFUL EVIL   CHAOTIC EVIL

OCCUPATION: _____

PORTRAIT

Roll In Story:
_____
_____
_____
_____
_____
_____
_____
_____
_____
_____
_____

Physical Description
_____
_____
_____
_____
_____

Personality
_____
_____
_____
_____
_____
_____
_____
_____

Discerning Features
_____
_____
_____
_____
_____

Unique Talents / Abilities:
_____
_____
_____
_____
_____

Character TRIGGER Questions:

- Is your character considered normal and acceptable in this society? Why not?
- Does your character have any mannerisms, habits or desires considered taboo?
- What does your character do that causes others to feel uncomfortable?
- Does he / she have any special needs that have to be met (such as medication or therapy)?
- Does your character have an unknown connection to a famous / infamous person or group in history?
- Does your character have a deep secret that could change the course of events?
- What are your characters core beliefs ? Name three (3) principles they will not compromise.

- What is the greatest loss your character has experienced?
- What is your characters greatest fear? How does that affect the way they make decisions?
- What are your characters dreams? What we desire forms our decisions, so what does he / she want?
- Does your character have any specific prejudices? What are they and how do they affect interactions with others?
- Does he / she have an overpowering addiction considered a weakness...or perhaps a strength?
- Do they have a latent ability (or repressed memory) that can be brought out in the story?
- Is your character being used as a pawn in a much bigger plot behind the scenes?
- What lie have they told that will soon catch up & expose them?

FATHER:

MOTHER:

SIBLINGS:

FRIENDS:

HABITS / MANNERISMS

INTERNAL / EXTERNAL CONFLICTS:

PERSONAL STORY ARC

CHARACTER HISTORY

NAME [   ]   BOOK

NICKNAME [   ]   Series

IMPORTANCE				
COORDINATION				
INFLUENCE				
STRENGTH				
INTELLIGENCE				
WISDOM				
STREETWISE				
DIPLOMACY				
CHARISMA				
WILL				

Race: [   ]

Age: [   ]   Weight: [   ]

PORTRAIT

LAWFUL GOOD   CHAOTIC GOOD

N

LAWFUL EVIL   CHAOTIC EVIL

OCCUPATION: [   ]

Roll In Story:

_____

Physical Description

_____

Personality

_____

Discerning Features

_____

Unique Talents / Abilities:

_____

Character TRIGGER Questions:

- Is your character considered normal and acceptable in this society? Why not?
- Does your character have any mannerisms, habits or desires considered taboo?
- What does your character do that causes others to feel uncomfortable?
- Does he / she have any special needs that have to be met (such as medication or therapy)?
- Does your character have an unknown connection to a famous / infamous person or group in history?
- Does your character have a deep secret that could change the course of events?
- What are your characters core beliefs ? Name three (3) principles they will not compromise.

- What is the greatest loss your character has experienced?
- What is your characters greatest fear? How does that affect the way they make decisions?
- What are your characters dreams? What we desire forms our decisions, so what does he / she want?
- Does your character have any specific prejudices? What are they and how do they affect interactions with others?
- Does he / she have an overpowering addiction considered a weakness...or perhaps a strength?
- Do they have a latent ability (or repressed memory) that can be brought out in the story?
- Is your character being used as a pawn in a much bigger plot behind the scenes?
- What lie have they told that will soon catch up & expose them?

FATHER:

MOTHER:

SIBLINGS:

FRIENDS:

HABITS / MANNERISMS

INTERNAL / EXTERNAL CONFLICTS:

PERSONAL STORY ARC

CHARACTER HISTORY

NAME [_____] BOOK [_____]

NICKNAME [_____] Series [_____]

IMPORTANCE [__|__|__|__]
INFLUENCE [__|__|__|__]

STRENGTH [__|__|__|__]
COORDINATION [__|__|__|__]

INTELLIGENCE [__|__|__|__]
WISDOM [__|__|__|__]
STREETWISE [__|__|__|__]
DIPLOMACY [__|__|__|__]
CHARISMA [__|__|__|__]
WILL [__|__|__|__]

Race: [_____]

Age: [_____] Weight: [_____]

PORTRAIT

LAWFUL GOOD   CHAOTIC GOOD

N

LAWFUL EVIL   CHAOTIC EVIL

OCCUPATION: [_____]

Roll In Story:
_____
_____
_____
_____
_____
_____
_____
_____
_____
_____
_____
_____
_____

Physical Description
_____
_____
_____
_____
_____

Personality
_____
_____
_____
_____
_____
_____

Discerning Features
_____
_____
_____
_____

Unique Talents / Abilities:
_____
_____
_____
_____
_____

Character TRIGGER Questions:

- Is your character considered normal and acceptable in this society? Why not?
- Does your character have any mannerisms, habits or desires considered taboo?
- What does your character do that causes others to feel uncomfortable?
- Does he / she have any special needs that have to be met (such as medication or therapy)?
- Does your character have an unknown connection to a famous / infamous person or group in history?
- Does your character have a deep secret that could change the course of events?
- What are your characters core beliefs ? Name three (3) principles they will not compromise.

- What is the greatest loss your character has experienced?
- What is your characters greatest fear? How does that affect the way they make decisions?
- What are your characters dreams? What we desire forms our decisions, so what does he / she want?
- Does your character have any specific prejudices? What are they and how do they affect interactions with others?
- Does he / she have an overpowering addiction considered a weakness...or perhaps a strength?
- Do they have a latent ability (or repressed memory) that can be brought out in the story?
- Is your character being used as a pawn in a much bigger plot behind the scenes?
- What lie have they told that will soon catch up & expose them?

FATHER:

MOTHER:

SIBLINGS:

FRIENDS:

HABITS / MANNERISMS

INTERNAL / EXTERNAL CONFLICTS:

PERSONAL STORY ARC

CHARACTER HISTORY

NAME _____

NICKNAME _____

BOOK _____

Series _____

| IMPORTANCE | | | | |
| INFLUENCE | | | | |

| STRENGTH | | | | |
| COORDINATION | | | | |

INTELLIGENCE				
WISDOM				
STREETWISE				
DIPLOMACY				
CHARISMA				
WILL				

Race: _____

Age: _____   **Weight:** _____

LAWFUL GOOD		CHAOTIC GOOD
	N	
LAWFUL EVIL		CHAOTIC EVIL

OCCUPATION: _____

PORTRAIT

Roll In Story:

_____
_____
_____
_____
_____
_____
_____
_____
_____
_____
_____

Physical Description

_____
_____
_____
_____

Personality

_____
_____
_____
_____
_____

Discerning Features

_____
_____
_____
_____

Unique Talents / Abilities:

_____
_____
_____
_____

Character TRIGGER Questions:

-Is your character considered normal and acceptable in this society? Why not?
- Does your character have any mannerisms, habits or desires considered taboo?
- What does your character do that causes others to feel uncomfortable?
- Does he / she have any special needs that have to be met (such as medication or therapy)?
- Does your character have an unknown connection to a famous / infamous person or group in history?
- Does your character have a deep secret that could change the course of events?
- What are your characters core beliefs ? Name three (3) principles they will not compromise.

- What is the greatest loss your character has experienced?
- What is your characters greatest fear? How does that affect the way they make decisions?
- What are your characters dreams? What we desire forms our decisions, so what does he / she want?
- Does your character have any specific prejudices? What are they and how do they affect interactions with others?
- Does he / she have an overpowering addiction considered a weakness...or perhaps a strength?
- Do they have a latent ability (or repressed memory) that can be brought out in the story?
- Is your character being used as a pawn in a much bigger plot behind the scenes?
- What lie have they told that will soon catch up & expose them?

FATHER:

MOTHER:

SIBLINGS:

FRIENDS:

HABITS / MANNERISMS

INTERNAL / EXTERNAL CONFLICTS:

PERSONAL STORY ARC

CHARACTER HISTORY

NAME _____

NICKNAME _____

BOOK _____

Series _____

♂

♀

IMPORTANCE			
INFLUENCE			
STRENGTH			
COORDINATION			
INTELLIGENCE			
WISDOM			
STREETWISE			
DIPLOMACY			
CHARISMA			
WILL			

Race: _____

Age: _____ Weight: _____

LAWFUL GOOD   CHAOTIC GOOD

N

LAWFUL EVIL   CHAOTIC EVIL

OCCUPATION:

PORTRAIT

Roll In Story:

_____
_____
_____
_____
_____
_____
_____
_____
_____
_____
_____

Physical Description

_____
_____
_____
_____
_____

Personality

_____
_____
_____
_____
_____
_____
_____
_____
_____

Discerning Features

_____
_____
_____
_____
_____

Unique Talents / Abilities:

_____
_____
_____
_____
_____

Character TRIGGER Questions:

- Is your character considered normal and acceptable in this society? Why not?
- Does your character have any mannerisms, habits or desires considered taboo?
- What does your character do that causes others to feel uncomfortable?
- Does he / she have any special needs that have to be met (such as medication or therapy)?
- Does your character have an unknown connection to a famous / infamous person or group in history?
- Does your character have a deep secret that could change the course of events?
- What are your characters core beliefs ? Name three (3) principles they will not compromise.

- What is the greatest loss your character has experienced?
- What is your characters greatest fear? How does that affect the way they make decisions?
- What are your characters dreams? What we desire forms our decisions, so what does he / she want?
- Does your character have any specific prejudices? What are they and how do they affect interactions with others?
- Does he / she have an overpowering addiction considered a weakness...or perhaps a strength?
- Do they have a latent ability (or repressed memory) that can be brought out in the story?
- Is your character being used as a pawn in a much bigger plot behind the scenes?
- What lie have they told that will soon catch up & expose them?

FATHER:

MOTHER:

SIBLINGS:

FRIENDS:

HABITS / MANNERISMS

INTERNAL / EXTERNAL CONFLICTS:

PERSONAL STORY ARC

CHARACTER HISTORY

NAME _____ BOOK _____

NICKNAME _____ Series _____

�male♂
♀female

IMPORTANCE [ ] [ ] [ ] [ ]
INFLUENCE [ ] [ ] [ ]

STRENGTH [ ] [ ] [ ]
COORDINATION [ ] [ ] [ ]

INTELLIGENCE [ ] [ ] [ ]
WISDOM [ ] [ ] [ ]
STREETWISE [ ] [ ] [ ]
DIPLOMACY [ ] [ ] [ ]
CHARISMA [ ] [ ] [ ]
WILL [ ] [ ]

Race: _____

Age: _____ Weight: _____

LAWFUL   CHAOTIC
GOOD   GOOD

N

LAWFUL   CHAOTIC
EVIL   EVIL

OCCUPATION: _____

PORTRAIT

Roll In Story:
_____
_____
_____
_____
_____
_____
_____
_____
_____

Physical Description
_____
_____
_____
_____
_____

Personality
_____
_____
_____
_____
_____

Discerning Features
_____
_____
_____

Unique Talents / Abilities:
_____
_____
_____
_____

Character TRIGGER Questions:

-Is your character considered normal and acceptable in this society? Why not?
- Does your character have any mannerisms, habits or desires considered taboo?
- What does your character do that causes others to feel uncomfortable?
- Does he / she have any special needs that have to be met (such as medication or therapy)?
- Does your character have an unknown connection to a famous / infamous person or group in history?
- Does your character have a deep secret that could change the course of events?
- What are your characters core beliefs ? Name three (3) principles they will not compromise.

- What is the greatest loss your character has experienced?
- What is your characters greatest fear? How does that affect the way they make decisions?
- What are your characters dreams? What we desire forms our decisions, so what does he / she want?
- Does your character have any specific prejudices? What are they and how do they affect interactions with others?
- Does he / she have an overpowering addiction considered a weakness...or perhaps a strength?
- Do they have a latent ability (or repressed memory) that can be brought out in the story?
- Is your character being used as a pawn in a much bigger plot behind the scenes?
- What lie have they told that will soon catch up & expose them?

FATHER:

MOTHER:

SIBLINGS:

FRIENDS:

HABITS / MANNERISMS

INTERNAL / EXTERNAL CONFLICTS:

PERSONAL STORY ARC

CHARACTER HISTORY

NAME _____

NICKNAME _____

BOOK _____

Series _____

IMPORTANCE				
INFLUENCE				
STRENGTH				
COORDINATION				
INTELLIGENCE				
WISDOM				
STREETWISE				
DIPLOMACY				
CHARISMA				
WILL				

Race: _____

Age: _____ Weight: _____

PORTRAIT

LAWFUL GOOD   CHAOTIC GOOD

N

LAWFUL EVIL   CHAOTIC EVIL

OCCUPATION:

Roll In Story:

_____
_____
_____
_____
_____
_____
_____
_____
_____
_____

Physical Description

_____
_____
_____
_____
_____

Personality

_____
_____
_____
_____
_____
_____

Discerning Features

_____
_____
_____

Unique Talents / Abilities:

_____
_____
_____
_____

Character TRIGGER Questions:

-Is your character considered normal and acceptable in this society? Why not?
- Does your character have any mannerisms, habits or desires considered taboo?
- What does your character do that causes others to feel uncomfortable?
- Does he / she have any special needs that have to be met (such as medication or therapy)?
- Does your character have an unknown connection to a famous / infamous person or group in history?
- Does your character have a deep secret that could change the course of events?
- What are your characters core beliefs ? Name three (3) principles they will not compromise.

- What is the greatest loss your character has experienced?
- What is your characters greatest fear? How does that affect the way they make decisions?
- What are your characters dreams? What we desire forms our decisions, so what does he / she want?
- Does your character have any specific prejudices? What are they and how do they affect interactions with others?
- Does he / she have an overpowering addiction considered a weakness...or perhaps a strength?
- Do they have a latent ability (or repressed memory) that can be brought out in the story?
- Is your character being used as a pawn in a much bigger plot behind the scenes?
- What lie have they told that will soon catch up & expose them?

FATHER:

MOTHER:

SIBLINGS:

FRIENDS:

HABITS / MANNERISMS

INTERNAL / EXTERNAL CONFLICTS:

PERSONAL STORY ARC

CHARACTER HISTORY

NAME _____   BOOK _____

NICKNAME _____   Series _____

IMPORTANCE | | | |
INFLUENCE | | | |

STRENGTH | | | |
COORDINATION | | | |

INTELLIGENCE | | | |
WISDOM | | | |
STREETWISE | | | |
DIPLOMACY | | | |
CHARISMA | | | |
WILL | | | |

Race: _____

Age: _____   Weight: _____

PORTRAIT

LAWFUL   CHAOTIC
GOOD   GOOD

N

LAWFUL   CHAOTIC
EVIL   EVIL

OCCUPATION:

Roll In Story:

_____
_____
_____
_____
_____
_____
_____
_____
_____
_____
_____

Physical Description

_____
_____
_____
_____
_____

Personality

_____
_____
_____
_____
_____
_____
_____

Discerning Features

_____
_____
_____
_____

Unique Talents / Abilities:

_____
_____
_____
_____

Character TRIGGER Questions:

-Is your character considered normal and acceptable in this society? Why not?
- Does your character have any mannerisms, habits or desires considered taboo?
- What does your character do that causes others to feel uncomfortable?
- Does he / she have any special needs that have to be met (such as medication or therapy)?
- Does your character have an unknown connection to a famous / infamous person or group in history?
- Does your character have a deep secret that could change the course of events?
- What are your characters core beliefs ? Name three (3) principles they will not compromise.

- What is the greatest loss your character has experienced?
- What is your characters greatest fear? How does that affect the way they make decisions?
- What are your characters dreams? What we desire forms our decisions, so what does he / she want?
- Does your character have any specific prejudices? What are they and how do they affect interactions with others?
- Does he / she have an overpowering addiction considered a weakness...or perhaps a strength?
- Do they have a latent ability (or repressed memory) that can be brought out in the story?
- Is your character being used as a pawn in a much bigger plot behind the scenes?
- What lie have they told that will soon catch up & expose them?

FATHER:

MOTHER:

FRIENDS:

SIBLINGS:

HABITS / MANNERISMS

INTERNAL / EXTERNAL CONFLICTS:

PERSONAL STORY ARC

CHARACTER HISTORY

NAME _____

BOOK _____

NICKNAME _____

Series _____

IMPORTANCE				
INFLUENCE				
STRENGTH				
COORDINATION				
INTELLIGENCE				
WISDOM				
STREETWISE				
DIPLOMACY				
CHARISMA				
WILL				

Race: _____

Age: _____   Weight: _____

PORTRAIT

LAWFUL GOOD   CHAOTIC GOOD

N

LAWFUL EVIL   CHAOTIC EVIL

OCCUPATION: _____

Roll In Story:

_____
_____
_____
_____
_____
_____
_____
_____
_____
_____
_____

Physical Description

_____
_____
_____
_____

Personality

_____
_____
_____
_____
_____
_____

Discerning Features

_____
_____
_____
_____

Unique Talents / Abilities:

_____
_____
_____
_____

Character TRIGGER Questions:

-Is your character considered normal and acceptable in this society? Why not?

- Does your character have any mannerisms, habits or desires considered taboo?

- What does your character do that causes others to feel uncomfortable?

- Does he / she have any special needs that have to be met (such as medication or therapy)?

- Does your character have an unknown connection to a famous / infamous person or group in history?

- Does your character have a deep secret that could change the course of events?

- What are your characters core beliefs ? Name three (3) principles they will not compromise.

- What is the greatest loss your character has experienced?

- What is your characters greatest fear? How does that affect the way they make decisions?

- What are your characters dreams? What we desire forms our decisions, so what does he / she want?

- Does your character have any specific prejudices? What are they and how do they affect interactions with others?

- Does he / she have an overpowering addiction considered a weakness...or perhaps a strength?

- Do they have a latent ability (or repressed memory) that can be brought out in the story?

- Is your character being used as a pawn in a much bigger plot behind the scenes?

- What lie have they told that will soon catch up & expose them?

FATHER:

MOTHER:

SIBLINGS:

FRIENDS:

HABITS / MANNERISMS

INTERNAL / EXTERNAL CONFLICTS:

PERSONAL STORY ARC

CHARACTER HISTORY

NAME [   ]   BOOK [   ]

NICKNAME [   ]   Series [   ]

IMPORTANCE			
INFLUENCE			
STRENGTH			
COORDINATION			
INTELLIGENCE			
WISDOM			
STREETWISE			
DIPLOMACY			
CHARISMA			
WILL			

Race: [   ]

Age: [   ]   Weight: [   ]

PORTRAIT

LAWFUL GOOD   CHAOTIC GOOD

N

LAWFUL EVIL   CHAOTIC EVIL

OCCUPATION: [   ]

Roll In Story:

Physical Description

Personality

Discerning Features

Unique Talents / Abilities:

Character TRIGGER Questions:

-Is your character considered normal and acceptable in this society? Why not?
- Does your character have any mannerisms, habits or desires considered taboo?
- What does your character do that causes others to feel uncomfortable?
- Does he / she have any special needs that have to be met (such as medication or therapy)?
- Does your character have an unknown connection to a famous / infamous person or group in history?
- Does your character have a deep secret that could change the course of events?
- What are your characters core beliefs ? Name three (3) principles they will not compromise.

- What is the greatest loss your character has experienced?
- What is your characters greatest fear? How does that affect the way they make decisions?
- What are your characters dreams? What we desire forms our decisions, so what does he / she want?
- Does your character have any specific prejudices? What are they and how do they affect interactions with others?
- Does he / she have an overpowering addiction considered a weakness...or perhaps a strength?
- Do they have a latent ability (or repressed memory) that can be brought out in the story?
- Is your character being used as a pawn in a much bigger plot behind the scenes?
- What lie have they told that will soon catch up & expose them?

FATHER:

MOTHER:

SIBLINGS:

FRIENDS:

HABITS / MANNERISMS

INTERNAL / EXTERNAL CONFLICTS:

PERSONAL STORY ARC

CHARACTER HISTORY

NAME [   ] BOOK [   ]

NICKNAME [   ] Series [   ]

IMPORTANCE			
INFLUENCE			
STRENGTH			
COORDINATION			
INTELLIGENCE			
WISDOM			
STREETWISE			
DIPLOMACY			
CHARISMA			
WILL			

Race: [   ]

Age: [   ] Weight: [   ]

PORTRAIT

LAWFUL GOOD   CHAOTIC GOOD

N

LAWFUL EVIL   CHAOTIC EVIL

OCCUPATION: [   ]

Roll In Story:

_____
_____
_____
_____
_____
_____
_____
_____
_____
_____
_____

Physical Description

_____
_____
_____
_____
_____

Personality

_____
_____
_____
_____
_____
_____
_____
_____

Discerning Features

_____
_____
_____

Unique Talents / Abilities:

_____
_____
_____
_____
_____

Character TRIGGER Questions:

-Is your character considered normal and acceptable in this society? Why not?

- Does your character have any mannerisms, habits or desires considered taboo?

- What does your character do that causes others to feel uncomfortable?

- Does he / she have any special needs that have to be met (such as medication or therapy)?

- Does your character have an unknown connection to a famous / infamous person or group in history?

- Does your character have a deep secret that could change the course of events?

- What are your characters core beliefs? Name three (3) principles they will not compromise.

- What is the greatest loss your character has experienced?

- What is your characters greatest fear? How does that affect the way they make decisions?

- What are your characters dreams? What we desire forms our decisions, so what does he / she want?

- Does your character have any specific prejudices? What are they and how do they affect interactions with others?

- Does he / she have an overpowering addiction considered a weakness...or perhaps a strength?

- Do they have a latent ability (or repressed memory) that can be brought out in the story?

- Is your character being used as a pawn in a much bigger plot behind the scenes?

- What lie have they told that will soon catch up & expose them?

FATHER:

MOTHER:

SIBLINGS:

FRIENDS:

HABITS / MANNERISMS

INTERNAL / EXTERNAL CONFLICTS:

PERSONAL STORY ARC

CHARACTER HISTORY

NAME _____

NICKNAME _____

BOOK _____

Series _____

IMPORTANCE

INFLUENCE

STRENGTH

COORDINATION

INTELLIGENCE

WISDOM

STREETWISE

DIPLOMACY

CHARISMA

WILL

Race: _____

Age: _____ Weight: _____

LAWFUL GOOD   CHAOTIC GOOD

N

LAWFUL EVIL   CHAOTIC EVIL

OCCUPATION: _____

PORTRAIT

Roll In Story:

_____

Physical Description

_____

Personality

_____

Discerning Features

_____

Unique Talents / Abilities:

_____

Character TRIGGER Questions:

-Is your character considered normal and acceptable in this society? Why not?

- Does your character have any mannerisms, habits or desires considered taboo?

- What does your character do that causes others to feel uncomfortable?

- Does he / she have any special needs that have to be met (such as medication or therapy)?

- Does your character have an unknown connection to a famous / infamous person or group in history?

- Does your character have a deep secret that could change the course of events?

- What are your characters core beliefs ? Name three (3) principles they will not compromise.

- What is the greatest loss your character has experienced?

- What is your characters greatest fear? How does that affect the way they make decisions?

- What are your characters dreams? What we desire forms our decisions, so what does he / she want?

- Does your character have any specific prejudices? What are they and how do they affect interactions with others?

- Does he / she have an overpowering addiction considered a weakness...or perhaps a strength?

- Do they have a latent ability (or repressed memory) that can be brought out in the story?

- Is your character being used as a pawn in a much bigger plot behind the scenes?

- What lie have they told that will soon catch up & expose them?

FATHER:

MOTHER:

SIBLINGS:

FRIENDS:

HABITS / MANNERISMS

INTERNAL / EXTERNAL CONFLICTS:

PERSONAL STORY ARC

CHARACTER HISTORY

NAME _____   BOOK

NICKNAME _____   Series

IMPORTANCE | | | |
INFLUENCE | | | |

STRENGTH _____
COORDINATION _____

INTELLIGENCE _____
WISDOM _____
STREETWISE _____
DIPLOMACY _____
CHARISMA _____
WILL _____

Race:
_____

Age: _____   Weight: _____

LAWFUL GOOD   CHAOTIC GOOD

N

LAWFUL EVIL   CHAOTIC EVIL

OCCUPATION:
_____

PORTRAIT

Roll In Story:

_____
_____
_____
_____
_____
_____
_____
_____
_____
_____

Physical Description

_____
_____
_____
_____
_____

Personality

_____
_____
_____
_____
_____
_____

Discerning Features

_____
_____
_____
_____
_____

Unique Talents / Abilities:

_____
_____
_____
_____

Character TRIGGER Questions:

-Is your character considered normal and acceptable in this society? Why not?
- Does your character have any mannerisms, habits or desires considered taboo?
- What does your character do that causes others to feel uncomfortable?
- Does he / she have any special needs that have to be met (such as medication or therapy)?
- Does your character have an unknown connection to a famous / infamous person or group in history?
- Does your character have a deep secret that could change the course of events?
- What are your characters core beliefs? Name three (3) principles they will not compromise.

- What is the greatest loss your character has experienced?
- What is your characters greatest fear? How does that affect the way they make decisions?
- What are your characters dreams? What we desire forms our decisions, so what does he / she want?
- Does your character have any specific prejudices? What are they and how do they affect interactions with others?
- Does he / she have an overpowering addiction considered a weakness...or perhaps a strength?
- Do they have a latent ability (or repressed memory) that can be brought out in the story?
- Is your character being used as a pawn in a much bigger plot behind the scenes?
- What lie have they told that will soon catch up & expose them?

FATHER:

MOTHER:

SIBLINGS:

FRIENDS:

HABITS / MANNERISMS

INTERNAL / EXTERNAL CONFLICTS:

PERSONAL STORY ARC

CHARACTER HISTORY

NAME _____

NICKNAME _____

BOOK _____

Series _____

IMPORTANCE				
INFLUENCE				
STRENGTH				
COORDINATION				
INTELLIGENCE				
WISDOM				
STREETWISE				
DIPLOMACY				
CHARISMA				
WILL				

Race: _____

Age: _____   Weight: _____

LAWFUL GOOD   CHAOTIC GOOD

N

LAWFUL EVIL   CHAOTIC EVIL

OCCUPATION: _____

PORTRAIT

Roll In Story:
_____
_____
_____
_____
_____
_____
_____
_____
_____

Physical Description
_____
_____
_____
_____
_____

Personality
_____
_____
_____
_____
_____
_____
_____

Discerning Features
_____
_____
_____

Unique Talents / Abilities:
_____
_____
_____
_____

Character TRIGGER Questions:

-Is your character considered normal and acceptable in this society? Why not?
- Does your character have any mannerisms, habits or desires considered taboo?
- What does your character do that causes others to feel uncomfortable?
- Does he / she have any special needs that have to be met (such as medication or therapy)?
- Does your character have an unknown connection to a famous / infamous person or group in history?
- Does your character have a deep secret that could change the course of events?
- What are your characters core beliefs ? Name three (3) principles they will not compromise.

- What is the greatest loss your character has experienced?
- What is your characters greatest fear? How does that affect the way they make decisions?
- What are your characters dreams? What we desire forms our decisions, so what does he / she want?
- Does your character have any specific prejudices? What are they and how do they affect interactions with others?
- Does he / she have an overpowering addiction considered a weakness...or perhaps a strength?
- Do they have a latent ability (or repressed memory) that can be brought out in the story?
- Is your character being used as a pawn in a much bigger plot behind the scenes?
- What lie have they told that will soon catch up & expose them?

FATHER:

MOTHER:

SIBLINGS:

FRIENDS:

HABITS / MANNERISMS

INTERNAL / EXTERNAL CONFLICTS:

PERSONAL STORY ARC

CHARACTER HISTORY

NAME _____   BOOK _____

NICKNAME _____   Series _____

IMPORTANCE				
INFLUENCE				
STRENGTH				
COORDINATION				
INTELLIGENCE				
WISDOM				
STREETWISE				
DIPLOMACY				
CHARISMA				
WILL				

Race: _____

Age: ____   Weight: ____

PORTRAIT

LAWFUL GOOD .... CHAOTIC GOOD

N

LAWFUL EVIL .... CHAOTIC EVIL

OCCUPATION: _____

Roll In Story:

_____

Physical Description

_____

Personality

_____

Discerning Features

_____

Unique Talents / Abilities:

_____

Character TRIGGER Questions:

-Is your character considered normal and acceptable in this society? Why not?
- Does your character have any mannerisms, habits or desires considered taboo?
- What does your character do that causes others to feel uncomfortable?
- Does he / she have any special needs that have to be met (such as medication or therapy)?
- Does your character have an unknown connection to a famous / infamous person or group in history?
- Does your character have a deep secret that could change the course of events?
- What are your characters core beliefs ? Name three (3) principles they will not compromise.

- What is the greatest loss your character has experienced?
- What is your characters greatest fear? How does that affect the way they make decisions?
- What are your characters dreams? What we desire forms our decisions, so what does he / she want?
- Does your character have any specific prejudices? What are they and how do they affect interactions with others?
- Does he / she have an overpowering addiction considered a weakness...or perhaps a strength?
- Do they have a latent ability (or repressed memory) that can be brought out in the story?
- Is your character being used as a pawn in a much bigger plot behind the scenes?
- What lie have they told that will soon catch up & expose them?

FATHER:

MOTHER:

SIBLINGS:

FRIENDS:

HABITS / MANNERISMS

INTERNAL / EXTERNAL CONFLICTS:

PERSONAL STORY ARC

CHARACTER HISTORY

NAME _____

BOOK _____

NICKNAME _____

Series _____

IMPORTANCE [ ][ ][ ]

INFLUENCE [ ]

STRENGTH [ ]

COORDINATION [ ]

INTELLIGENCE [ ]

WISDOM [ ]

STREETWISE [ ]

DIPLOMACY [ ]

CHARISMA [ ]

WILL [ ]

Race: _____

PORTRAIT

Age: _____ Weight: _____

LAWFUL GOOD		CHAOTIC GOOD
	N	
LAWFUL EVIL		CHAOTIC EVIL

OCCUPATION: _____

Roll In Story:
_____
_____
_____
_____
_____
_____
_____
_____
_____
_____
_____
_____

Physical Description
_____
_____
_____
_____
_____

Personality
_____
_____
_____
_____
_____
_____
_____

Discerning Features
_____
_____
_____
_____

Unique Talents / Abilities:
_____
_____
_____
_____
_____

Character TRIGGER Questions:

- Is your character considered normal and acceptable in this society? Why not?
- Does your character have any mannerisms, habits or desires considered taboo?
- What does your character do that causes others to feel uncomfortable?
- Does he / she have any special needs that have to be met (such as medication or therapy)?
- Does your character have an unknown connection to a famous / infamous person or group in history?
- Does your character have a deep secret that could change the course of events?
- What are your characters core beliefs? Name three (3) principles they will not compromise.

- What is the greatest loss your character has experienced?
- What is your characters greatest fear? How does that affect the way they make decisions?
- What are your characters dreams? What we desire forms our decisions, so what does he / she want?
- Does your character have any specific prejudices? What are they and how do they affect interactions with others?
- Does he / she have an overpowering addiction considered a weakness...or perhaps a strength?
- Do they have a latent ability (or repressed memory) that can be brought out in the story?
- Is your character being used as a pawn in a much bigger plot behind the scenes?
- What lie have they told that will soon catch up & expose them?

FATHER:

MOTHER:

SIBLINGS:

FRIENDS:

HABITS / MANNERISMS

INTERNAL / EXTERNAL CONFLICTS:

PERSONAL STORY ARC

CHARACTER HISTORY

NAME _____   **BOOK** _____

NICKNAME _____   **Series** _____

♂

IMPORTANCE				
INFLUENCE				
STRENGTH				
COORDINATION				
INTELLIGENCE				
WISDOM				
STREETWISE				
DIPLOMACY				
CHARISMA				
WILL				

♀

Race: _____

Age: _____   Weight: _____

PORTRAIT

LAWFUL GOOD   CHAOTIC GOOD

N

LAWFUL EVIL   CHAOTIC EVIL

OCCUPATION: _____

Roll In Story:

_____
_____
_____
_____
_____
_____
_____
_____
_____
_____
_____
_____
_____

Physical Description

_____
_____
_____
_____
_____
_____
_____

Personality

_____
_____
_____
_____
_____
_____

Discerning Features

_____
_____
_____
_____

Unique Talents / Abilities:

_____
_____
_____
_____

Character TRIGGER Questions:

- Is your character considered normal and acceptable in this society? Why not?
- Does your character have any mannerisms, habits or desires considered taboo?
- What does your character do that causes others to feel uncomfortable?
- Does he / she have any special needs that have to be met (such as medication or therapy)?
- Does your character have an unknown connection to a famous / infamous person or group in history?
- Does your character have a deep secret that could change the course of events?
- What are your characters core beliefs ? Name three (3) principles they will not compromise.

- What is the greatest loss your character has experienced?
- What is your characters greatest fear? How does that affect the way they make decisions?
- What are your characters dreams? What we desire forms our decisions, so what does he / she want?
- Does your character have any specific prejudices? What are they and how do they affect interactions with others?
- Does he / she have an overpowering addiction considered a weakness...or perhaps a strength?
- Do they have a latent ability (or repressed memory) that can be brought out in the story?
- Is your character being used as a pawn in a much bigger plot behind the scenes?
- What lie have they told that will soon catch up & expose them?

FATHER:

MOTHER:

SIBLINGS:

FRIENDS:

HABITS / MANNERISMS

INTERNAL / EXTERNAL CONFLICTS:

PERSONAL STORY ARC

CHARACTER HISTORY

NAME _____ BOOK _____

NICKNAME _____ Series _____

IMPORTANCE ☐ ☐ ☐ ☐
INFLUENCE ☐ ☐ ☐

STRENGTH ☐ ☐ ☐
COORDINATION ☐ ☐ ☐

INTELLIGENCE ☐ ☐ ☐
WISDOM ☐ ☐ ☐
STREETWISE ☐ ☐ ☐
DIPLOMACY ☐ ☐ ☐
CHARISMA ☐ ☐ ☐
WILL ☐ ☐ ☐

Race: _____

Age: _____ Weight: _____

PORTRAIT

LAWFUL GOOD   CHAOTIC GOOD

N

LAWFUL EVIL   CHAOTIC EVIL

OCCUPATION: _____

Roll In Story:

_____
_____
_____
_____
_____
_____
_____
_____
_____
_____

Physical Description

_____
_____
_____
_____
_____
_____

Personality

_____
_____
_____
_____
_____
_____
_____
_____
_____
_____

Discerning Features

_____
_____
_____
_____
_____

Unique Talents / Abilities:

_____
_____
_____
_____
_____

Character TRIGGER Questions:

-Is your character considered normal and acceptable in this society? Why not?
- Does your character have any mannerisms, habits or desires considered taboo?
- What does your character do that causes others to feel uncomfortable?
- Does he / she have any special needs that have to be met (such as medication or therapy)?
- Does your character have an unknown connection to a famous / infamous person or group in history?
- Does your character have a deep secret that could change the course of events?
- What are your characters core beliefs ? Name three (3) principles they will not compromise.

- What is the greatest loss your character has experienced?
- What is your characters greatest fear? How does that affect the way they make decisions?
- What are your characters dreams? What we desire forms our decisions, so what does he / she want?
- Does your character have any specific prejudices? What are they and how do they affect interactions with others?
- Does he / she have an overpowering addiction considered a weakness...or perhaps a strength?
- Do they have a latent ability (or repressed memory) that can be brought out in the story?
- Is your character being used as a pawn in a much bigger plot behind the scenes?
- What lie have they told that will soon catch up & expose them?

FATHER:

MOTHER:

SIBLINGS:

FRIENDS:

HABITS / MANNERISMS

INTERNAL / EXTERNAL CONFLICTS:

PERSONAL STORY ARC

CHARACTER HISTORY

NAME _____ BOOK _____

NICKNAME _____ Series _____

IMPORTANCE [ ][ ][ ]
INFLUENCE [ ][ ][ ]

STRENGTH [ ][ ][ ]
COORDINATION [ ][ ][ ]

INTELLIGENCE [ ][ ][ ]
WISDOM [ ][ ][ ]
STREETWISE [ ][ ][ ]
DIPLOMACY [ ][ ][ ]
CHARISMA [ ][ ][ ]
WILL [ ][ ][ ]

Race: _____

Age: _____   Weight: _____

PORTRAIT

LAWFUL GOOD   CHAOTIC GOOD

N

LAWFUL EVIL   CHAOTIC EVIL

OCCUPATION: _____

Roll In Story:
_____
_____
_____
_____
_____
_____
_____
_____
_____
_____
_____
_____

Physical Description
_____
_____
_____
_____
_____

Personality
_____
_____
_____
_____
_____
_____

Discerning Features
_____
_____
_____

Unique Talents / Abilities:
_____
_____
_____
_____
_____

Character TRIGGER Questions:

-Is your character considered normal and acceptable in this society? Why not?
- Does your character have any mannerisms, habits or desires considered taboo?
- What does your character do that causes others to feel uncomfortable?
- Does he / she have any special needs that have to be met (such as medication or therapy)?
- Does your character have an unknown connection to a famous / infamous person or group in history?
- Does your character have a deep secret that could change the course of events?
- What are your characters core beliefs ? Name three (3) principles they will not compromise.

- What is the greatest loss your character has experienced?
- What is your characters greatest fear? How does that affect the way they make decisions?
- What are your characters dreams? What we desire forms our decisions, so what does he / she want?
- Does your character have any specific prejudices? What are they and how do they affect interactions with others?
- Does he / she have an overpowering addiction considered a weakness...or perhaps a strength?
- Do they have a latent ability (or repressed memory) that can be brought out in the story?
- Is your character being used as a pawn in a much bigger plot behind the scenes?
- What lie have they told that will soon catch up & expose them?

FATHER:

MOTHER:

SIBLINGS:

FRIENDS:

HABITS / MANNERISMS

INTERNAL / EXTERNAL CONFLICTS:

PERSONAL STORY ARC

CHARACTER HISTORY

NAME _____   BOOK _____

NICKNAME _____   Series _____

IMPORTANCE				
INFLUENCE				
STRENGTH				
COORDINATION				
INTELLIGENCE				
WISDOM				
STREETWISE				
DIPLOMACY				
CHARISMA				
WILL				

Race: _____

Age: _____   Weight: _____

LAWFUL GOOD   CHAOTIC GOOD

N

LAWFUL EVIL   CHAOTIC EVIL

OCCUPATION:

PORTRAIT

Roll In Story:

_____
_____
_____
_____
_____
_____
_____
_____
_____
_____
_____

Physical Description

_____
_____
_____
_____
_____
_____

Personality

_____
_____
_____
_____
_____
_____
_____

Discerning Features

_____
_____
_____

Unique Talents / Abilities:

_____
_____
_____
_____

Character TRIGGER Questions:

-Is your character considered normal and acceptable in this society? Why not?

- Does your character have any mannerisms, habits or desires considered taboo?

- What does your character do that causes others to feel uncomfortable?

- Does he / she have any special needs that have to be met (such as medication or therapy)?

- Does your character have an unknown connection to a famous / infamous person or group in history?

- Does your character have a deep secret that could change the course of events?

- What are your characters core beliefs ? Name three (3) principles they will not compromise.

- What is the greatest loss your character has experienced?

- What is your characters greatest fear? How does that affect the way they make decisions?

- What are your characters dreams? What we desire forms our decisions, so what does he / she want?

- Does your character have any specific prejudices? What are they and how do they affect interactions with others?

- Does he / she have an overpowering addiction considered a weakness...or perhaps a strength?

- Do they have a latent ability (or repressed memory) that can be brought out in the story?

- Is your character being used as a pawn in a much bigger plot behind the scenes?

- What lie have they told that will soon catch up & expose them?

FATHER:

MOTHER:

SIBLINGS:

FRIENDS:

HABITS / MANNERISMS

INTERNAL / EXTERNAL CONFLICTS:

PERSONAL STORY ARC

CHARACTER HISTORY

NAME _____ BOOK _____

NICKNAME _____ Series _____

IMPORTANCE				
INFLUENCE				
STRENGTH				
COORDINATION				
INTELLIGENCE				
WISDOM				
STREETWISE				
DIPLOMACY				
CHARISMA				
WILL				

Race: _____

Age: _____   Weight: _____

LAWFUL GOOD   CHAOTIC GOOD

N

LAWFUL EVIL   CHAOTIC EVIL

PORTRAIT

OCCUPATION: _____

Roll In Story:
_____
_____
_____
_____
_____
_____
_____
_____
_____
_____

Physical Description
_____
_____
_____
_____

Personality
_____
_____
_____
_____
_____
_____
_____

Discerning Features
_____
_____
_____
_____

Unique Talents / Abilities:
_____
_____
_____
_____

Character TRIGGER Questions:

-Is your character considered normal and acceptable in this society? Why not?

- Does your character have any mannerisms, habits or desires considered taboo?

- What does your character do that causes others to feel uncomfortable?

- Does he / she have any special needs that have to be met (such as medication or therapy)?

- Does your character have an unknown connection to a famous / infamous person or group in history?

- Does your character have a deep secret that could change the course of events?

- What are your characters core beliefs ? Name three (3) principles they will not compromise.

- What is the greatest loss your character has experienced?

- What is your characters greatest fear? How does that affect the way they make decisions?

- What are your characters dreams? What we desire forms our decisions, so what does he / she want?

- Does your character have any specific prejudices? What are they and how do they affect interactions with others?

- Does he / she have an overpowering addiction considered a weakness...or perhaps a strength?

- Do they have a latent ability (or repressed memory) that can be brought out in the story?

- Is your character being used as a pawn in a much bigger plot behind the scenes?

- What lie have they told that will soon catch up & expose them?

FATHER:

MOTHER:

SIBLINGS:

FRIENDS:

HABITS / MANNERISMS

INTERNAL / EXTERNAL CONFLICTS:

PERSONAL STORY ARC

CHARACTER HISTORY

NAME _____

NICKNAME _____

BOOK _____

Series _____

IMPORTANCE			
INFLUENCE			
STRENGTH			
COORDINATION			
INTELLIGENCE			
WISDOM			
STREETWISE			
DIPLOMACY			
CHARISMA			
WILL			

Race: _____

Age: _____   Weight: _____

PORTRAIT

LAWFUL GOOD   CHAOTIC GOOD

N

LAWFUL EVIL   CHAOTIC EVIL

OCCUPATION:

Roll In Story:

_____
_____
_____
_____
_____
_____
_____
_____
_____
_____
_____
_____

Physical Description

_____
_____
_____
_____

Personality

_____
_____
_____
_____
_____
_____

Discerning Features

_____
_____
_____

Unique Talents / Abilities:

_____
_____
_____
_____

Character TRIGGER Questions:

- Is your character considered normal and acceptable in this society? Why not?
- Does your character have any mannerisms, habits or desires considered taboo?
- What does your character do that causes others to feel uncomfortable?
- Does he / she have any special needs that have to be met (such as medication or therapy)?
- Does your character have an unknown connection to a famous / infamous person or group in history?
- Does your character have a deep secret that could change the course of events?
- What are your characters core beliefs ? Name three (3) principles they will not compromise.

- What is the greatest loss your character has experienced?
- What is your characters greatest fear? How does that affect the way they make decisions?
- What are your characters dreams? What we desire forms our decisions, so what does he / she want?
- Does your character have any specific prejudices? What are they and how do they affect interactions with others?
- Does he / she have an overpowering addiction considered a weakness...or perhaps a strength?
- Do they have a latent ability (or repressed memory) that can be brought out in the story?
- Is your character being used as a pawn in a much bigger plot behind the scenes?
- What lie have they told that will soon catch up & expose them?

FATHER:

MOTHER:

SIBLINGS:

FRIENDS:

HABITS / MANNERISMS

INTERNAL / EXTERNAL CONFLICTS:

PERSONAL STORY ARC

CHARACTER HISTORY

NAME _____

NICKNAME _____

BOOK _____

Series _____

IMPORTANCE	
INFLUENCE	
STRENGTH	
COORDINATION	
INTELLIGENCE	
WISDOM	
STREETWISE	
DIPLOMACY	
CHARISMA	
WILL	

Race: _____

Age: _____   **Weight:** _____

LAWFUL GOOD   CHAOTIC GOOD

N

LAWFUL EVIL   CHAOTIC EVIL

OCCUPATION: _____

PORTRAIT

Roll In Story:

_____
_____
_____
_____
_____
_____
_____
_____
_____
_____
_____
_____

Physical Description

_____
_____
_____
_____

Personality

_____
_____
_____
_____
_____
_____
_____

Discerning Features

_____
_____

Unique Talents / Abilities:

_____
_____
_____
_____
_____

Character TRIGGER Questions:

- Is your character considered normal and acceptable in this society? Why not?
- Does your character have any mannerisms, habits or desires considered taboo?
- What does your character do that causes others to feel uncomfortable?
- Does he / she have any special needs that have to be met (such as medication or therapy)?
- Does your character have an unknown connection to a famous / infamous person or group in history?
- Does your character have a deep secret that could change the course of events?
- What are your characters core beliefs ? Name three (3) principles they will not compromise.

- What is the greatest loss your character has experienced?
- What is your characters greatest fear? How does that affect the way they make decisions?
- What are your characters dreams? What we desire forms our decisions, so what does he / she want?
- Does your character have any specific prejudices? What are they and how do they affect interactions with others?
- Does he / she have an overpowering addiction considered a weakness...or perhaps a strength?
- Do they have a latent ability (or repressed memory) that can be brought out in the story?
- Is your character being used as a pawn in a much bigger plot behind the scenes?
- What lie have they told that will soon catch up & expose them?

FATHER:

MOTHER:

SIBLINGS:

FRIENDS:

HABITS / MANNERISMS

INTERNAL / EXTERNAL CONFLICTS:

PERSONAL STORY ARC

CHARACTER HISTORY

NAME _____   **BOOK** _____

NICKNAME _____   **Series** _____

IMPORTANCE [ ][ ][ ][ ]
INFLUENCE [ ][ ][ ][ ]
STRENGTH [ ][ ][ ][ ]
COORDINATION [ ][ ][ ][ ]
INTELLIGENCE [ ][ ][ ][ ]
WISDOM [ ][ ][ ][ ]
STREETWISE [ ][ ][ ][ ]
DIPLOMACY [ ][ ][ ][ ]
CHARISMA [ ][ ][ ][ ]
WILL [ ][ ][ ][ ]

Race: _____

Age: _____   Weight: _____

LAWFUL GOOD		CHAOTIC GOOD
	N	
LAWFUL EVIL		CHAOTIC EVIL

PORTRAIT

Roll In Story:
_____
_____
_____
_____
_____
_____
_____
_____
_____
_____
_____
_____
_____

OCCUPATION: _____

Physical Description
_____
_____
_____
_____
_____

Personality
_____
_____
_____
_____
_____
_____
_____
_____

Discerning Features
_____
_____
_____
_____

Unique Talents / Abilities:
_____
_____
_____
_____

Character TRIGGER Questions:

-Is your character considered normal and acceptable in this society? Why not?
- Does your character have any mannerisms, habits or desires considered taboo?
- What does your character do that causes others to feel uncomfortable?
- Does he / she have any special needs that have to be met (such as medication or therapy)?
- Does your character have an unknown connection to a famous / infamous person or group in history?
- Does your character have a deep secret that could change the course of events?
- What are your characters core beliefs ? Name three (3) principles they will not compromise.

- What is the greatest loss your character has experienced?
- What is your characters greatest fear? How does that affect the way they make decisions?
- What are your characters dreams? What we desire forms our decisions, so what does he / she want?
- Does your character have any specific prejudices? What are they and how do they affect interactions with others?
- Does he / she have an overpowering addiction considered a weakness...or perhaps a strength?
- Do they have a latent ability (or repressed memory) that can be brought out in the story?
- Is your character being used as a pawn in a much bigger plot behind the scenes?
- What lie have they told that will soon catch up & expose them?

FATHER:

MOTHER:

SIBLINGS:

FRIENDS:

HABITS / MANNERISMS

INTERNAL / EXTERNAL CONFLICTS:

PERSONAL STORY ARC

CHARACTER HISTORY

NAME [   ] **BOOK** [   ]

NICKNAME [   ] **Series** [   ]

IMPORTANCE			
INFLUENCE			
STRENGTH			
COORDINATION			
INTELLIGENCE			
WISDOM			
STREETWISE			
DIPLOMACY			
CHARISMA			
WILL			

Race: [   ]

Age: [   ] **Weight:** [   ]

PORTRAIT

LAWFUL GOOD   CHAOTIC GOOD

N

LAWFUL EVIL   CHAOTIC EVIL

OCCUPATION: [   ]

Roll In Story:

_____
_____
_____
_____
_____
_____
_____
_____
_____
_____
_____

Physical Description

_____
_____
_____
_____
_____
_____
_____

Personality

_____
_____
_____
_____
_____
_____
_____

Discerning Features

_____
_____
_____

Unique Talents / Abilities:

_____
_____
_____
_____
_____

Character TRIGGER Questions:

-Is your character considered normal and acceptable in this society? Why not?

- Does your character have any mannerisms, habits or desires considered taboo?

- What does your character do that causes others to feel uncomfortable?

- Does he / she have any special needs that have to be met (such as medication or therapy)?

- Does your character have an unknown connection to a famous / infamous person or group in history?

- Does your character have a deep secret that could change the course of events?

- What are your characters core beliefs ? Name three (3) principles they will not compromise.

- What is the greatest loss your character has experienced?

- What is your characters greatest fear? How does that affect the way they make decisions?

- What are your characters dreams? What we desire forms our decisions, so what does he / she want?

- Does your character have any specific prejudices? What are they and how do they affect interactions with others?

- Does he / she have an overpowering addiction considered a weakness...or perhaps a strength?

- Do they have a latent ability (or repressed memory) that can be brought out in the story?

- Is your character being used as a pawn in a much bigger plot behind the scenes?

- What lie have they told that will soon catch up & expose them?

FATHER:

MOTHER:

SIBLINGS:

FRIENDS:

HABITS / MANNERISMS

INTERNAL / EXTERNAL CONFLICTS:

PERSONAL STORY ARC

CHARACTER HISTORY

NAME _____

NICKNAME _____

BOOK _____

Series _____

IMPORTANCE				
INFLUENCE				

STRENGTH	
COORDINATION	

INTELLIGENCE	
WISDOM	
STREETWISE	
DIPLOMACY	
CHARISMA	
WILL	

Race: _____

Age: _____ Weight: _____

PORTRAIT

LAWFUL GOOD   CHAOTIC GOOD

N

LAWFUL EVIL   CHAOTIC EVIL

OCCUPATION:

Roll In Story:

_____
_____
_____
_____
_____
_____
_____
_____
_____
_____
_____
_____

Personality

_____
_____
_____
_____
_____
_____

Physical Description

_____
_____
_____
_____

Discerning Features

_____
_____
_____

Unique Talents / Abilities:

_____
_____
_____
_____

Character TRIGGER Questions:

- Is your character considered normal and acceptable in this society? Why not?
- Does your character have any mannerisms, habits or desires considered taboo?
- What does your character do that causes others to feel uncomfortable?
- Does he / she have any special needs that have to be met (such as medication or therapy)?
- Does your character have an unknown connection to a famous / infamous person or group in history?
- Does your character have a deep secret that could change the course of events?
- What are your characters core beliefs ? Name three (3) principles they will not compromise.

- What is the greatest loss your character has experienced?
- What is your characters greatest fear? How does that affect the way they make decisions?
- What are your characters dreams? What we desire forms our decisions, so what does he / she want?
- Does your character have any specific prejudices? What are they and how do they affect interactions with others?
- Does he / she have an overpowering addiction considered a weakness...or perhaps a strength?
- Do they have a latent ability (or repressed memory) that can be brought out in the story?
- Is your character being used as a pawn in a much bigger plot behind the scenes?
- What lie have they told that will soon catch up & expose them?

FATHER:

MOTHER:

SIBLINGS:

FRIENDS:

HABITS / MANNERISMS

INTERNAL / EXTERNAL CONFLICTS:

PERSONAL STORY ARC

CHARACTER HISTORY

NAME _____ BOOK

NICKNAME _____ Series

IMPORTANCE			
INFLUENCE			
STRENGTH			
COORDINATION			
INTELLIGENCE			
WISDOM			
STREETWISE			
DIPLOMACY			
CHARISMA			
WILL			

Race:

Age: Weight:

PORTRAIT

```
LAWFUL                    CHAOTIC
GOOD                        GOOD

              N

LAWFUL                    CHAOTIC
EVIL                        EVIL
```

OCCUPATION:

Roll In Story:

_____
_____
_____
_____
_____
_____
_____
_____
_____
_____
_____

Physical Description

_____
_____
_____
_____
_____

Personality

_____
_____
_____
_____
_____
_____

Discerning Features

_____
_____
_____
_____

Unique Talents / Abilities:

_____
_____
_____
_____

Character TRIGGER Questions:

-Is your character considered normal and acceptable in this society? Why not?
- Does your character have any mannerisms, habits or desires considered taboo?
- What does your character do that causes others to feel uncomfortable?
- Does he / she have any special needs that have to be met (such as medication or therapy)?
- Does your character have an unknown connection to a famous / infamous person or group in history?
- Does your character have a deep secret that could change the course of events?
- What are your characters core beliefs ? Name three (3) principles they will not compromise.

- What is the greatest loss your character has experienced?
- What is your characters greatest fear? How does that affect the way they make decisions?
- What are your characters dreams? What we desire forms our decisions, so what does he / she want?
- Does your character have any specific prejudices? What are they and how do they affect interactions with others?
- Does he / she have an overpowering addiction considered a weakness...or perhaps a strength?
- Do they have a latent ability (or repressed memory) that can be brought out in the story?
- Is your character being used as a pawn in a much bigger plot behind the scenes?
- What lie have they told that will soon catch up & expose them?

FATHER:

MOTHER:

SIBLINGS:

FRIENDS:

HABITS / MANNERISMS

INTERNAL / EXTERNAL CONFLICTS:

PERSONAL STORY ARC

CHARACTER HISTORY

NAME

NICKNAME

BOOK

Series

IMPORTANCE

INFLUENCE

STRENGTH

COORDINATION

INTELLIGENCE

WISDOM

STREETWISE

DIPLOMACY

CHARISMA

WILL

Race:

Age: Weight:

LAWFUL   CHAOTIC
GOOD   GOOD

N

LAWFUL   CHAOTIC
EVIL   EVIL

OCCUPATION:

PORTRAIT

Roll In Story:

Physical Description

Personality

Discerning Features

Unique Talents / Abilities:

Character TRIGGER Questions:

-Is your character considered normal and acceptable
  in this society? Why not?
- Does your character have any mannerisms, habits
  or desires considered taboo?
- What does your character do that causes others to
  feel uncomfortable?
- Does he / she have any special needs that have to
  be met (such as medication or therapy)?
- Does your character have an unknown connection
  to a famous / infamous person or group in history?
- Does your character have a deep secret that could
  change the course of events?
- What are your characters core beliefs ? Name three (3)
  principles they will not compromise.

- What is the greatest loss your character has experienced?
- What is your characters greatest fear? How does that affect
  the way they make decisions?
- What are your characters dreams? What we desire forms
  our decisions, so what does he / she want?
- Does your character have any specific prejudices? What are
  they and how do they affect interactions with others?
- Does he / she have an overpowering addiction considered a
  weakness...or perhaps a strength?
- Do they have a latent ability (or repressed memory) that
  can be brought out in the story?
- Is your character being used as a pawn in a much bigger plot
  behind the scenes?
- What lie have they told that will soon catch up & expose them?

FATHER:

MOTHER:

SIBLINGS:

FRIENDS:

HABITS / MANNERISMS

INTERNAL / EXTERNAL CONFLICTS:

PERSONAL STORY ARC

CHARACTER HISTORY

NAME _____   BOOK _____

NICKNAME _____   Series _____

IMPORTANCE	
INFLUENCE	
STRENGTH	
COORDINATION	
INTELLIGENCE	
WISDOM	
STREETWISE	
DIPLOMACY	
CHARISMA	
WILL	

Race: _____

Age: _____   Weight: _____

LAWFUL GOOD   CHAOTIC GOOD

N

LAWFUL EVIL   CHAOTIC EVIL

OCCUPATION: _____

PORTRAIT

Roll In Story:

_____
_____
_____
_____
_____
_____
_____
_____
_____
_____
_____

Physical Description

_____
_____
_____

Personality

_____
_____
_____
_____
_____
_____
_____

Discerning Features

_____
_____
_____

Unique Talents / Abilities:

_____
_____
_____
_____

Character TRIGGER Questions:

- Is your character considered normal and acceptable in this society? Why not?
- Does your character have any mannerisms, habits or desires considered taboo?
- What does your character do that causes others to feel uncomfortable?
- Does he / she have any special needs that have to be met (such as medication or therapy)?
- Does your character have an unknown connection to a famous / infamous person or group in history?
- Does your character have a deep secret that could change the course of events?
- What are your characters core beliefs? Name three (3) principles they will not compromise.

- What is the greatest loss your character has experienced?
- What is your characters greatest fear? How does that affect the way they make decisions?
- What are your characters dreams? What we desire forms our decisions, so what does he / she want?
- Does your character have any specific prejudices? What are they and how do they affect interactions with others?
- Does he / she have an overpowering addiction considered a weakness...or perhaps a strength?
- Do they have a latent ability (or repressed memory) that can be brought out in the story?
- Is your character being used as a pawn in a much bigger plot behind the scenes?
- What lie have they told that will soon catch up & expose them?

FATHER:

MOTHER:

SIBLINGS:

FRIENDS:

HABITS / MANNERISMS

INTERNAL / EXTERNAL CONFLICTS:

PERSONAL STORY ARC

CHARACTER HISTORY

NAME _____ BOOK _____

NICKNAME _____ Series _____

IMPORTANCE	
INFLUENCE	
STRENGTH	
COORDINATION	
INTELLIGENCE	
WISDOM	
STREETWISE	
DIPLOMACY	
CHARISMA	
WILL	

Race: _____

Age: _____ Weight: _____

LAWFUL GOOD   CHAOTIC GOOD

N

LAWFUL EVIL   CHAOTIC EVIL

OCCUPATION: _____

PORTRAIT

Roll In Story:

_____
_____
_____
_____
_____
_____
_____
_____
_____
_____

Physical Description

_____
_____
_____
_____
_____

Personality

_____
_____
_____
_____
_____
_____

Discerning Features

_____
_____
_____
_____

Unique Talents / Abilities:

_____
_____
_____
_____
_____

Character TRIGGER Questions:

-Is your character considered normal and acceptable in this society? Why not?
- Does your character have any mannerisms, habits or desires considered taboo?
- What does your character do that causes others to feel uncomfortable?
- Does he / she have any special needs that have to be met (such as medication or therapy)?
- Does your character have an unknown connection to a famous / infamous person or group in history?
- Does your character have a deep secret that could change the course of events?
- What are your characters core beliefs ? Name three (3) principles they will not compromise.

- What is the greatest loss your character has experienced?
- What is your characters greatest fear? How does that affect the way they make decisions?
- What are your characters dreams? What we desire forms our decisions, so what does he / she want?
- Does your character have any specific prejudices? What are they and how do they affect interactions with others?
- Does he / she have an overpowering addiction considered a weakness...or perhaps a strength?
- Do they have a latent ability (or repressed memory) that can be brought out in the story?
- Is your character being used as a pawn in a much bigger plot behind the scenes?
- What lie have they told that will soon catch up & expose them?

FATHER:

MOTHER:

SIBLINGS:

FRIENDS:

HABITS / MANNERISMS

INTERNAL / EXTERNAL CONFLICTS:

PERSONAL STORY ARC

CHARACTER HISTORY

NAME _____

NICKNAME _____

BOOK _____

Series _____

IMPORTANCE				
INFLUENCE				
STRENGTH				
COORDINATION				
INTELLIGENCE				
WISDOM				
STREETWISE				
DIPLOMACY				
CHARISMA				
WILL				

Race: _____

Age: _____ Weight: _____

PORTRAIT

LAWFUL
GOOD

CHAOTIC
GOOD

N

LAWFUL
EVIL

CHAOTIC
EVIL

OCCUPATION: _____

Roll In Story:

_____
_____
_____
_____
_____
_____
_____
_____
_____
_____
_____
_____
_____
_____

Physical Description

_____
_____
_____
_____
_____

Personality

_____
_____
_____
_____
_____
_____
_____

Discerning Features

_____
_____
_____
_____
_____

Unique Talents / Abilities:

_____
_____
_____
_____
_____

Character TRIGGER Questions:

-Is your character considered normal and acceptable in this society? Why not?

- Does your character have any mannerisms, habits or desires considered taboo?

- What does your character do that causes others to feel uncomfortable?

- Does he / she have any special needs that have to be met (such as medication or therapy)?

- Does your character have an unknown connection to a famous / infamous person or group in history?

- Does your character have a deep secret that could change the course of events?

- What are your characters core beliefs ? Name three (3) principles they will not compromise.

- What is the greatest loss your character has experienced?

- What is your characters greatest fear? How does that affect the way they make decisions?

- What are your characters dreams? What we desire forms our decisions, so what does he / she want?

- Does your character have any specific prejudices? What are they and how do they affect interactions with others?

- Does he / she have an overpowering addiction considered a weakness...or perhaps a strength?

- Do they have a latent ability (or repressed memory) that can be brought out in the story?

- Is your character being used as a pawn in a much bigger plot behind the scenes?

- What lie have they told that will soon catch up & expose them?

FATHER:

MOTHER:

SIBLINGS:

FRIENDS:

HABITS / MANNERISMS

INTERNAL / EXTERNAL CONFLICTS:

PERSONAL STORY ARC

CHARACTER HISTORY

NAME _____

NICKNAME _____

BOOK _____

Series _____

IMPORTANCE [ ][ ][ ][ ]
INFLUENCE [ ][ ][ ][ ]
STRENGTH [ ][ ][ ][ ]
COORDINATION [ ][ ][ ][ ]
INTELLIGENCE [ ][ ][ ][ ]
WISDOM [ ][ ][ ][ ]
STREETWISE [ ][ ][ ][ ]
DIPLOMACY [ ][ ][ ][ ]
CHARISMA [ ][ ][ ][ ]
WILL [ ]

Race: _____

Age: _____ Weight: _____

LAWFUL GOOD   CHAOTIC GOOD

N

LAWFUL EVIL   CHAOTIC EVIL

OCCUPATION: _____

PORTRAIT

Roll In Story:

_____
_____
_____
_____
_____
_____
_____
_____
_____
_____

Physical Description

_____
_____
_____

Personality

_____
_____
_____
_____
_____
_____
_____

Discerning Features

_____
_____

Unique Talents / Abilities:

_____
_____
_____
_____
_____

Character TRIGGER Questions:

-Is your character considered normal and acceptable in this society? Why not?
- Does your character have any mannerisms, habits or desires considered taboo?
- What does your character do that causes others to feel uncomfortable?
- Does he / she have any special needs that have to be met (such as medication or therapy)?
- Does your character have an unknown connection to a famous / infamous person or group in history?
- Does your character have a deep secret that could change the course of events?
- What are your characters core beliefs ? Name three (3) principles they will not compromise.

- What is the greatest loss your character has experienced?
- What is your characters greatest fear? How does that affect the way they make decisions?
- What are your characters dreams? What we desire forms our decisions, so what does he / she want?
- Does your character have any specific prejudices? What are they and how do they affect interactions with others?
- Does he / she have an overpowering addiction considered a weakness...or perhaps a strength?
- Do they have a latent ability (or repressed memory) that can be brought out in the story?
- Is your character being used as a pawn in a much bigger plot behind the scenes?
- What lie have they told that will soon catch up & expose them?

FATHER:

MOTHER:

SIBLINGS:

FRIENDS:

HABITS / MANNERISMS

INTERNAL / EXTERNAL CONFLICTS:

PERSONAL STORY ARC

CHARACTER HISTORY

NAME

NICKNAME

BOOK

Series

IMPORTANCE

INFLUENCE

STRENGTH

COORDINATION

INTELLIGENCE

WISDOM

STREETWISE

DIPLOMACY

CHARISMA

WILL

Race:

Age: Weight:

LAWFUL   CHAOTIC
GOOD   GOOD

N

LAWFUL   CHAOTIC
EVIL   EVIL

OCCUPATION:

PORTRAIT

Roll In Story:

Physical Description

Personality

Discerning Features

Unique Talents / Abilities:

Character TRIGGER Questions:

-Is your character considered normal and acceptable
  in this society? Why not?
- Does your character have any mannerisms, habits
  or desires considered taboo?
- What does your character do that causes others to
  feel uncomfortable?
- Does he / she have any special needs that have to
  be met (such as medication or therapy)?
- Does your character have an unknown connection
  to a famous / infamous person or group in history?
- Does your character have a deep secret that could
  change the course of events?
- What are your characters core beliefs ? Name three (3)
  principles they will not compromise.

- What is the greatest loss your character has experienced?
- What is your characters greatest fear? How does that affect
  the way they make decisions?
- What are your characters dreams? What we desire forms
  our decisions, so what does he / she want?
- Does your character have any specific prejudices? What are
  they and how do they affect interactions with others?
- Does he / she have an overpowering addiction considered a
  weakness...or perhaps a strength?
- Do they have a latent ability (or repressed memory) that
  can be brought out in the story?
- Is your character being used as a pawn in a much bigger plot
  behind the scenes?
- What lie have they told that will soon catch up & expose them?

FATHER:

MOTHER:

SIBLINGS:

FRIENDS:

HABITS / MANNERISMS

INTERNAL / EXTERNAL CONFLICTS:

PERSONAL STORY ARC

CHARACTER HISTORY

NAME _____   BOOK _____

NICKNAME _____   Series _____

IMPORTANCE			
INFLUENCE			
STRENGTH			
COORDINATION			
INTELLIGENCE			
WISDOM			
STREETWISE			
DIPLOMACY			
CHARISMA			
WILL			

Race: _____

Age: _____   Weight: _____

PORTRAIT

LAWFUL GOOD   CHAOTIC GOOD

N

LAWFUL EVIL   CHAOTIC EVIL

OCCUPATION: _____

Roll In Story:

_____
_____
_____
_____
_____
_____
_____
_____
_____
_____
_____
_____

Physical Description

_____
_____
_____
_____

Personality

_____
_____
_____
_____
_____
_____
_____

Discerning Features

_____
_____
_____
_____

Unique Talents / Abilities:

_____
_____
_____
_____

Character TRIGGER Questions:

-Is your character considered normal and acceptable in this society? Why not?

- Does your character have any mannerisms, habits or desires considered taboo?

- What does your character do that causes others to feel uncomfortable?

- Does he / she have any special needs that have to be met (such as medication or therapy)?

- Does your character have an unknown connection to a famous / infamous person or group in history?

- Does your character have a deep secret that could change the course of events?

- What are your characters core beliefs ? Name three (3) principles they will not compromise.

- What is the greatest loss your character has experienced?

- What is your characters greatest fear? How does that affect the way they make decisions?

- What are your characters dreams? What we desire forms our decisions, so what does he / she want?

- Does your character have any specific prejudices? What are they and how do they affect interactions with others?

- Does he / she have an overpowering addiction considered a weakness...or perhaps a strength?

- Do they have a latent ability (or repressed memory) that can be brought out in the story?

- Is your character being used as a pawn in a much bigger plot behind the scenes?

- What lie have they told that will soon catch up & expose them?

FATHER:

MOTHER:

SIBLINGS:

FRIENDS:

HABITS / MANNERISMS

INTERNAL / EXTERNAL CONFLICTS:

PERSONAL STORY ARC

CHARACTER HISTORY

NAME _____   BOOK _____

NICKNAME _____   Series _____

IMPORTANCE | | | | |
INFLUENCE | | | | |

STRENGTH | |
COORDINATION | |

INTELLIGENCE | |
WISDOM | |
STREETWISE | |
DIPLOMACY | |
CHARISMA | |
WILL | |

Race: _____

Age: _____   Weight: _____

PORTRAIT

LAWFUL GOOD .... CHAOTIC GOOD

N

LAWFUL EVIL .... CHAOTIC EVIL

OCCUPATION:

Roll In Story:

_____
_____
_____
_____
_____
_____
_____
_____

Physical Description

_____
_____
_____
_____
_____

Personality

_____
_____
_____
_____
_____
_____

Discerning Features

_____
_____
_____
_____

Unique Talents / Abilities:

_____
_____
_____
_____

Character TRIGGER Questions:

-Is your character considered normal and acceptable in this society? Why not?
- Does your character have any mannerisms, habits or desires considered taboo?
- What does your character do that causes others to feel uncomfortable?
- Does he / she have any special needs that have to be met (such as medication or therapy)?
- Does your character have an unknown connection to a famous / infamous person or group in history?
- Does your character have a deep secret that could change the course of events?
- What are your characters core beliefs ? Name three (3) principles they will not compromise.

- What is the greatest loss your character has experienced?
- What is your characters greatest fear? How does that affect the way they make decisions?
- What are your characters dreams? What we desire forms our decisions, so what does he / she want?
- Does your character have any specific prejudices? What are they and how do they affect interactions with others?
- Does he / she have an overpowering addiction considered a weakness...or perhaps a strength?
- Do they have a latent ability (or repressed memory) that can be brought out in the story?
- Is your character being used as a pawn in a much bigger plot behind the scenes?
- What lie have they told that will soon catch up & expose them?

FATHER:

MOTHER:

SIBLINGS:

FRIENDS:

HABITS / MANNERISMS

INTERNAL / EXTERNAL CONFLICTS:

PERSONAL STORY ARC

CHARACTER HISTORY

NAME _____ BOOK _____

NICKNAME _____ Series _____

IMPORTANCE	
INFLUENCE	
STRENGTH	
COORDINATION	
INTELLIGENCE	
WISDOM	
STREETWISE	
DIPLOMACY	
CHARISMA	
WILL	

Race: _____

Age: _____ Weight: _____

LAWFUL GOOD   CHAOTIC GOOD

N

LAWFUL EVIL   CHAOTIC EVIL

PORTRAIT

OCCUPATION:

Roll In Story:

_____
_____
_____
_____
_____
_____
_____
_____
_____
_____
_____
_____
_____

Physical Description

_____
_____
_____
_____
_____
_____

Personality

_____
_____
_____
_____
_____
_____
_____

Discerning Features

_____
_____
_____
_____

Unique Talents / Abilities:

_____
_____
_____
_____

Character TRIGGER Questions:

- Is your character considered normal and acceptable in this society? Why not?
- Does your character have any mannerisms, habits or desires considered taboo?
- What does your character do that causes others to feel uncomfortable?
- Does he / she have any special needs that have to be met (such as medication or therapy)?
- Does your character have an unknown connection to a famous / infamous person or group in history?
- Does your character have a deep secret that could change the course of events?
- What are your characters core beliefs ? Name three (3) principles they will not compromise.

- What is the greatest loss your character has experienced?
- What is your characters greatest fear? How does that affect the way they make decisions?
- What are your characters dreams? What we desire forms our decisions, so what does he / she want?
- Does your character have any specific prejudices? What are they and how do they affect interactions with others?
- Does he / she have an overpowering addiction considered a weakness...or perhaps a strength?
- Do they have a latent ability (or repressed memory) that can be brought out in the story?
- Is your character being used as a pawn in a much bigger plot behind the scenes?
- What lie have they told that will soon catch up & expose them?

FATHER:

MOTHER:

SIBLINGS:

FRIENDS:

HABITS / MANNERISMS

INTERNAL / EXTERNAL CONFLICTS:

PERSONAL STORY ARC

CHARACTER HISTORY

NAME

NICKNAME

BOOK

Series

IMPORTANCE				
INFLUENCE				
STRENGTH				
COORDINATION				
INTELLIGENCE				
WISDOM				
STREETWISE				
DIPLOMACY				
CHARISMA				
WILL				

Race:

Age:

Weight:

PORTRAIT

LAWFUL
GOOD

CHAOTIC
GOOD

N

LAWFUL
EVIL

CHAOTIC
EVIL

OCCUPATION:

Roll In Story:

Physical Description

Personality

Discerning Features

Unique Talents / Abilities:

Character TRIGGER Questions:

-Is your character considered normal and acceptable in this society? Why not?

- Does your character have any mannerisms, habits or desires considered taboo?

- What does your character do that causes others to feel uncomfortable?

- Does he / she have any special needs that have to be met (such as medication or therapy)?

- Does your character have an unknown connection to a famous / infamous person or group in history?

- Does your character have a deep secret that could change the course of events?

- What are your characters core beliefs ? Name three (3) principles they will not compromise.

- What is the greatest loss your character has experienced?

- What is your characters greatest fear? How does that affect the way they make decisions?

- What are your characters dreams? What we desire forms our decisions, so what does he / she want?

- Does your character have any specific prejudices? What are they and how do they affect interactions with others?

- Does he / she have an overpowering addiction considered a weakness...or perhaps a strength?

- Do they have a latent ability (or repressed memory) that can be brought out in the story?

- Is your character being used as a pawn in a much bigger plot behind the scenes?

- What lie have they told that will soon catch up & expose them?

FATHER:

MOTHER:

SIBLINGS:

FRIENDS:

HABITS / MANNERISMS

INTERNAL / EXTERNAL CONFLICTS:

PERSONAL STORY ARC

CHARACTER HISTORY

NAME **_____**   BOOK

NICKNAME **_____**   Series

IMPORTANCE				
INFLUENCE				
STRENGTH				
COORDINATION				
INTELLIGENCE				
WISDOM				
STREETWISE				
DIPLOMACY				
CHARISMA				
WILL				

Race: _____

Age: _____   Weight: _____

PORTRAIT

LAWFUL GOOD   CHAOTIC GOOD

N

LAWFUL EVIL   CHAOTIC EVIL

OCCUPATION:

Roll In Story:

_____
_____
_____
_____
_____
_____
_____
_____
_____
_____
_____
_____
_____
_____
_____
_____

Physical Description

_____
_____
_____
_____
_____
_____

Personality

_____
_____
_____
_____
_____
_____
_____
_____

Discerning Features

_____
_____
_____
_____
_____
_____

Unique Talents / Abilities:

_____
_____
_____
_____

Character TRIGGER Questions:

-Is your character considered normal and acceptable
   in this society? Why not?
- Does your character have any mannerisms, habits
   or desires considered taboo?
- What does your character do that causes others to
   feel uncomfortable?
- Does he / she have any special needs that have to
   be met (such as medication or therapy)?
- Does your character have an unknown connection
   to a famous / infamous person or group in history?
- Does your character have a deep secret that could
   change the course of events?
- What are your characters core beliefs ? Name three (3)
   principles they will not compromise.

- What is the greatest loss your character has experienced?
- What is your characters greatest fear? How does that affect
   the way they make decisions?
- What are your characters dreams? What we desire forms
   our decisions, so what does he / she want?
- Does your character have any specific prejudices? What are
   they and how do they affect interactions with others?
- Does he / she have an overpowering addiction considered a
   weakness...or perhaps a strength?
- Do they have a latent ability (or repressed memory) that
   can be brought out in the story?
- Is your character being used as a pawn in a much bigger plot
   behind the scenes?
- What lie have they told that will soon catch up & expose them?

FATHER:

MOTHER:

SIBLINGS:

FRIENDS:

HABITS / MANNERISMS

INTERNAL / EXTERNAL CONFLICTS:

PERSONAL STORY ARC

CHARACTER HISTORY

NAME

NICKNAME

BOOK

Series

IMPORTANCE			
INFLUENCE			
STRENGTH			
COORDINATION			
INTELLIGENCE			
WISDOM			
STREETWISE			
DIPLOMACY			
CHARISMA			
WILL			

Race:

Age: Weight:

LAWFUL GOOD   CHAOTIC GOOD

N

LAWFUL EVIL   CHAOTIC EVIL

OCCUPATION:

PORTRAIT

Roll In Story:

Physical Description

Personality

Discerning Features

Unique Talents / Abilities:

Character TRIGGER Questions:

- Is your character considered normal and acceptable in this society? Why not?
- Does your character have any mannerisms, habits or desires considered taboo?
- What does your character do that causes others to feel uncomfortable?
- Does he / she have any special needs that have to be met (such as medication or therapy)?
- Does your character have an unknown connection to a famous / infamous person or group in history?
- Does your character have a deep secret that could change the course of events?
- What are your characters core beliefs ? Name three (3) principles they will not compromise.

- What is the greatest loss your character has experienced?
- What is your characters greatest fear? How does that affect the way they make decisions?
- What are your characters dreams? What we desire forms our decisions, so what does he / she want?
- Does your character have any specific prejudices? What are they and how do they affect interactions with others?
- Does he / she have an overpowering addiction considered a weakness...or perhaps a strength?
- Do they have a latent ability (or repressed memory) that can be brought out in the story?
- Is your character being used as a pawn in a much bigger plot behind the scenes?
- What lie have they told that will soon catch up & expose them?

FATHER:

MOTHER:

SIBLINGS:

FRIENDS:

HABITS / MANNERISMS

INTERNAL / EXTERNAL CONFLICTS:

PERSONAL STORY ARC

CHARACTER HISTORY

NAME [_____]   **BOOK** [_____]

NICKNAME [_____]   **Series** [_____]

IMPORTANCE	
INFLUENCE	
STRENGTH	
COORDINATION	
INTELLIGENCE	
WISDOM	
STREETWISE	
DIPLOMACY	
CHARISMA	
WILL	

Race: [_____]

Age: [_____]   Weight: [_____]

PORTRAIT

LAWFUL GOOD ———— CHAOTIC GOOD

N

LAWFUL EVIL ———— CHAOTIC EVIL

OCCUPATION: [_____]

Roll In Story:
_____
_____
_____
_____
_____
_____
_____
_____
_____
_____
_____
_____
_____

Physical Description
_____
_____
_____
_____
_____

Personality
_____
_____
_____
_____
_____
_____

Discerning Features
_____
_____
_____
_____
_____

Unique Talents / Abilities:
_____
_____
_____
_____
_____

Character TRIGGER Questions:

- Is your character considered normal and acceptable in this society? Why not?
- Does your character have any mannerisms, habits or desires considered taboo?
- What does your character do that causes others to feel uncomfortable?
- Does he / she have any special needs that have to be met (such as medication or therapy)?
- Does your character have an unknown connection to a famous / infamous person or group in history?
- Does your character have a deep secret that could change the course of events?
- What are your characters core beliefs ? Name three (3) principles they will not compromise.

- What is the greatest loss your character has experienced?
- What is your characters greatest fear? How does that affect the way they make decisions?
- What are your characters dreams? What we desire forms our decisions, so what does he / she want?
- Does your character have any specific prejudices? What are they and how do they affect interactions with others?
- Does he / she have an overpowering addiction considered a weakness...or perhaps a strength?
- Do they have a latent ability (or repressed memory) that can be brought out in the story?
- Is your character being used as a pawn in a much bigger plot behind the scenes?
- What lie have they told that will soon catch up & expose them?

FATHER:

MOTHER:

SIBLINGS:

FRIENDS:

HABITS / MANNERISMS

INTERNAL / EXTERNAL CONFLICTS:

PERSONAL STORY ARC

CHARACTER HISTORY

NAME [ ] BOOK

NICKNAME [ ] Series

IMPORTANCE [ ][ ][ ][ ] Race: [ ]

INFLUENCE [ ][ ][ ][ ]

STRENGTH [ ] Age: [ ] Weight: [ ]

COORDINATION [ ]

INTELLIGENCE [ ]

WISDOM [ ]

STREETWISE [ ]

DIPLOMACY [ ]

CHARISMA [ ]

WILL [ ]

Roll In Story:

LAWFUL GOOD .... CHAOTIC GOOD

N

LAWFUL EVIL .... CHAOTIC EVIL

OCCUPATION: [ ]

PORTRAIT [ ]

Physical Description

_____

Personality

_____

Discerning Features

_____

Unique Talents / Abilities:

_____

Character TRIGGER Questions:

-Is your character considered normal and acceptable in this society? Why not?

- Does your character have any mannerisms, habits or desires considered taboo?

- What does your character do that causes others to feel uncomfortable?

- Does he / she have any special needs that have to be met (such as medication or therapy)?

- Does your character have an unknown connection to a famous / infamous person or group in history?

- Does your character have a deep secret that could change the course of events?

- What are your characters core beliefs ? Name three (3) principles they will not compromise.

- What is the greatest loss your character has experienced?

- What is your characters greatest fear? How does that affect the way they make decisions?

- What are your characters dreams? What we desire forms our decisions, so what does he / she want?

- Does your character have any specific prejudices? What are they and how do they affect interactions with others?

- Does he / she have an overpowering addiction considered a weakness...or perhaps a strength?

- Do they have a latent ability (or repressed memory) that can be brought out in the story?

- Is your character being used as a pawn in a much bigger plot behind the scenes?

- What lie have they told that will soon catch up & expose them?

FATHER:

MOTHER:

SIBLINGS:

FRIENDS:

HABITS / MANNERISMS

INTERNAL / EXTERNAL CONFLICTS:

PERSONAL STORY ARC

CHARACTER HISTORY

NAME _____ BOOK _____

NICKNAME _____ Series _____

IMPORTANCE				
INFLUENCE				
STRENGTH				
COORDINATION				
INTELLIGENCE				
WISDOM				
STREETWISE				
DIPLOMACY				
CHARISMA				
WILL				

Race: _____

Age: _____ Weight: _____

PORTRAIT

LAWFUL GOOD   CHAOTIC GOOD

N

LAWFUL EVIL   CHAOTIC EVIL

OCCUPATION:

Roll In Story:
_____
_____
_____
_____
_____
_____
_____
_____
_____
_____
_____
_____

Physical Description
_____
_____
_____
_____
_____

Personality
_____
_____
_____
_____
_____
_____
_____

Discerning Features
_____
_____
_____
_____

Unique Talents / Abilities:
_____
_____
_____
_____

Character TRIGGER Questions:

- Is your character considered normal and acceptable in this society? Why not?
- Does your character have any mannerisms, habits or desires considered taboo?
- What does your character do that causes others to feel uncomfortable?
- Does he / she have any special needs that have to be met (such as medication or therapy)?
- Does your character have an unknown connection to a famous / infamous person or group in history?
- Does your character have a deep secret that could change the course of events?
- What are your characters core beliefs ? Name three (3) principles they will not compromise.

- What is the greatest loss your character has experienced?
- What is your characters greatest fear? How does that affect the way they make decisions?
- What are your characters dreams? What we desire forms our decisions, so what does he / she want?
- Does your character have any specific prejudices? What are they and how do they affect interactions with others?
- Does he / she have an overpowering addiction considered a weakness...or perhaps a strength?
- Do they have a latent ability (or repressed memory) that can be brought out in the story?
- Is your character being used as a pawn in a much bigger plot behind the scenes?
- What lie have they told that will soon catch up & expose them?

FATHER:

MOTHER:

SIBLINGS:

FRIENDS:

HABITS / MANNERISMS

INTERNAL / EXTERNAL CONFLICTS:

PERSONAL STORY ARC

CHARACTER HISTORY

NAME _____

NICKNAME _____

BOOK _____

Series _____

IMPORTANCE	
INFLUENCE	
STRENGTH	
COORDINATION	
INTELLIGENCE	
WISDOM	
STREETWISE	
DIPLOMACY	
CHARISMA	
WILL	

Race: _____

Age: _____ **Weight:** _____

LAWFUL GOOD   CHAOTIC GOOD

N

LAWFUL EVIL   CHAOTIC EVIL

OCCUPATION:

PORTRAIT

Roll In Story:

_____
_____
_____
_____
_____
_____
_____
_____
_____
_____
_____
_____

Personality

_____
_____
_____
_____
_____
_____
_____
_____

Physical Description

_____
_____
_____
_____
_____

Discerning Features

_____
_____
_____
_____
_____

Unique Talents / Abilities:

_____
_____
_____
_____

Character TRIGGER Questions:

-Is your character considered normal and acceptable in this society? Why not?

- Does your character have any mannerisms, habits or desires considered taboo?

- What does your character do that causes others to feel uncomfortable?

- Does he / she have any special needs that have to be met (such as medication or therapy)?

- Does your character have an unknown connection to a famous / infamous person or group in history?

- Does your character have a deep secret that could change the course of events?

- What are your characters core beliefs ? Name three (3) principles they will not compromise.

- What is the greatest loss your character has experienced?

- What is your characters greatest fear? How does that affect the way they make decisions?

- What are your characters dreams? What we desire forms our decisions, so what does he / she want?

- Does your character have any specific prejudices? What are they and how do they affect interactions with others?

- Does he / she have an overpowering addiction considered a weakness...or perhaps a strength?

- Do they have a latent ability (or repressed memory) that can be brought out in the story?

- Is your character being used as a pawn in a much bigger plot behind the scenes?

- What lie have they told that will soon catch up & expose them?

FATHER:

MOTHER:

SIBLINGS:

FRIENDS:

HABITS / MANNERISMS

INTERNAL / EXTERNAL CONFLICTS:

PERSONAL STORY ARC

CHARACTER HISTORY

NAME _____

NICKNAME _____

BOOK _____

Series _____

IMPORTANCE				
INFLUENCE				
STRENGTH				
COORDINATION				
INTELLIGENCE				
WISDOM				
STREETWISE				
DIPLOMACY				
CHARISMA				
WILL				

Race: _____

Age: _____ Weight: _____

LAWFUL GOOD .... CHAOTIC GOOD

N

LAWFUL EVIL .... CHAOTIC EVIL

OCCUPATION: _____

PORTRAIT

Roll In Story:

_____

Physical Description

_____

Personality

_____

Discerning Features

_____

Unique Talents / Abilities:

_____

Character TRIGGER Questions:

- Is your character considered normal and acceptable in this society? Why not?
- Does your character have any mannerisms, habits or desires considered taboo?
- What does your character do that causes others to feel uncomfortable?
- Does he / she have any special needs that have to be met (such as medication or therapy)?
- Does your character have an unknown connection to a famous / infamous person or group in history?
- Does your character have a deep secret that could change the course of events?
- What are your characters core beliefs ? Name three (3) principles they will not compromise.

- What is the greatest loss your character has experienced?
- What is your characters greatest fear? How does that affect the way they make decisions?
- What are your characters dreams? What we desire forms our decisions, so what does he / she want?
- Does your character have any specific prejudices? What are they and how do they affect interactions with others?
- Does he / she have an overpowering addiction considered a weakness...or perhaps a strength?
- Do they have a latent ability (or repressed memory) that can be brought out in the story?
- Is your character being used as a pawn in a much bigger plot behind the scenes?
- What lie have they told that will soon catch up & expose them?

FATHER:

MOTHER:

SIBLINGS:

FRIENDS:

HABITS / MANNERISMS

INTERNAL / EXTERNAL CONFLICTS:

PERSONAL STORY ARC

CHARACTER HISTORY

NAME _____

NICKNAME _____

BOOK _____

Series _____

IMPORTANCE			
INFLUENCE			
STRENGTH			
COORDINATION			
INTELLIGENCE			
WISDOM			
STREETWISE			
DIPLOMACY			
CHARISMA			
WILL			

Race: _____

Age: _____

Weight: _____

PORTRAIT

LAWFUL GOOD   CHAOTIC GOOD

N

LAWFUL EVIL   CHAOTIC EVIL

OCCUPATION: _____

Roll In Story:
_____
_____
_____
_____
_____
_____
_____
_____
_____
_____
_____
_____
_____
_____

Physical Description
_____
_____
_____
_____
_____
_____

Discerning Features
_____
_____
_____
_____
_____

Personality
_____
_____
_____
_____
_____
_____
_____

Unique Talents / Abilities:
_____
_____
_____
_____
_____

Character TRIGGER Questions:

-Is your character considered normal and acceptable in this society? Why not?

- Does your character have any mannerisms, habits or desires considered taboo?

- What does your character do that causes others to feel uncomfortable?

- Does he / she have any special needs that have to be met (such as medication or therapy)?

- Does your character have an unknown connection to a famous / infamous person or group in history?

- Does your character have a deep secret that could change the course of events?

- What are your characters core beliefs ? Name three (3) principles they will not compromise.

- What is the greatest loss your character has experienced?

- What is your characters greatest fear? How does that affect the way they make decisions?

- What are your characters dreams? What we desire forms our decisions, so what does he / she want?

- Does your character have any specific prejudices? What are they and how do they affect interactions with others?

- Does he / she have an overpowering addiction considered a weakness...or perhaps a strength?

- Do they have a latent ability (or repressed memory) that can be brought out in the story?

- Is your character being used as a pawn in a much bigger plot behind the scenes?

- What lie have they told that will soon catch up & expose them?

FATHER:

MOTHER:

SIBLINGS:

FRIENDS:

HABITS / MANNERISMS

INTERNAL / EXTERNAL CONFLICTS:

PERSONAL STORY ARC

CHARACTER HISTORY

NAME _____

NICKNAME _____

BOOK _____

Series _____

IMPORTANCE	
INFLUENCE	
STRENGTH	
COORDINATION	
INTELLIGENCE	
WISDOM	
STREETWISE	
DIPLOMACY	
CHARISMA	
WILL	

Race: _____

Age: _____   Weight: _____

LAWFUL GOOD   CHAOTIC GOOD

N

LAWFUL EVIL   CHAOTIC EVIL

OCCUPATION:

PORTRAIT

Roll In Story:
_____
_____
_____
_____
_____
_____
_____
_____
_____
_____
_____
_____
_____

Physical Description
_____
_____
_____
_____
_____
_____

Personality
_____
_____
_____
_____
_____
_____
_____

Discerning Features
_____
_____
_____
_____

Unique Talents / Abilities:
_____
_____
_____
_____
_____

Character TRIGGER Questions:

-Is your character considered normal and acceptable in this society? Why not?

- Does your character have any mannerisms, habits or desires considered taboo?

- What does your character do that causes others to feel uncomfortable?

- Does he / she have any special needs that have to be met (such as medication or therapy)?

- Does your character have an unknown connection to a famous / infamous person or group in history?

- Does your character have a deep secret that could change the course of events?

- What are your characters core beliefs ? Name three (3) principles they will not compromise.

- What is the greatest loss your character has experienced?

- What is your characters greatest fear? How does that affect the way they make decisions?

- What are your characters dreams? What we desire forms our decisions, so what does he / she want?

- Does your character have any specific prejudices? What are they and how do they affect interactions with others?

- Does he / she have an overpowering addiction considered a weakness...or perhaps a strength?

- Do they have a latent ability (or repressed memory) that can be brought out in the story?

- Is your character being used as a pawn in a much bigger plot behind the scenes?

- What lie have they told that will soon catch up & expose them?

FATHER:

MOTHER:

SIBLINGS:

FRIENDS:

HABITS / MANNERISMS

INTERNAL / EXTERNAL CONFLICTS:

PERSONAL STORY ARC

CHARACTER HISTORY

NAME

NICKNAME

BOOK

Series

	IMPORTANCE				
	INFLUENCE				
	STRENGTH				
	COORDINATION				
	INTELLIGENCE				
	WISDOM				
	STREETWISE				
	DIPLOMACY				
	CHARISMA				
	WILL				

Race:

Age:

Weight:

PORTRAIT

LAWFUL GOOD   CHAOTIC GOOD

N

LAWFUL EVIL   CHAOTIC EVIL

OCCUPATION:

Roll In Story:

Physical Description

Personality

Discerning Features

Unique Talents / Abilities:

Character TRIGGER Questions:

-Is your character considered normal and acceptable in this society? Why not?

- Does your character have any mannerisms, habits or desires considered taboo?

- What does your character do that causes others to feel uncomfortable?

- Does he / she have any special needs that have to be met (such as medication or therapy)?

- Does your character have an unknown connection to a famous / infamous person or group in history?

- Does your character have a deep secret that could change the course of events?

- What are your characters core beliefs ? Name three (3) principles they will not compromise.

- What is the greatest loss your character has experienced?

- What is your characters greatest fear? How does that affect the way they make decisions?

- What are your characters dreams? What we desire forms our decisions, so what does he / she want?

- Does your character have any specific prejudices? What are they and how do they affect interactions with others?

- Does he / she have an overpowering addiction considered a weakness...or perhaps a strength?

- Do they have a latent ability (or repressed memory) that can be brought out in the story?

- Is your character being used as a pawn in a much bigger plot behind the scenes?

- What lie have they told that will soon catch up & expose them?

FATHER:

MOTHER:

SIBLINGS:

FRIENDS:

HABITS / MANNERISMS

INTERNAL / EXTERNAL CONFLICTS:

PERSONAL STORY ARC

CHARACTER HISTORY

NAME _____ BOOK _____

NICKNAME _____ Series _____

IMPORTANCE				
INFLUENCE				
STRENGTH				
COORDINATION				
INTELLIGENCE				
WISDOM				
STREETWISE				
DIPLOMACY				
CHARISMA				
WILL				

Race: _____

Age: _____ Weight: _____

PORTRAIT

LAWFUL GOOD   CHAOTIC GOOD

N

LAWFUL EVIL   CHAOTIC EVIL

OCCUPATION: _____

Roll In Story:
_____
_____
_____
_____
_____
_____
_____
_____
_____
_____
_____
_____

Physical Description
_____
_____
_____
_____
_____

Personality
_____
_____
_____
_____
_____
_____
_____

Discerning Features
_____
_____
_____
_____

Unique Talents / Abilities:
_____
_____
_____
_____

Character TRIGGER Questions:

-Is your character considered normal and acceptable in this society? Why not?

- Does your character have any mannerisms, habits or desires considered taboo?

- What does your character do that causes others to feel uncomfortable?

- Does he / she have any special needs that have to be met (such as medication or therapy)?

- Does your character have an unknown connection to a famous / infamous person or group in history?

- Does your character have a deep secret that could change the course of events?

- What are your characters core beliefs ? Name three (3) principles they will not compromise.

- What is the greatest loss your character has experienced?

- What is your characters greatest fear? How does that affect the way they make decisions?

- What are your characters dreams? What we desire forms our decisions, so what does he / she want?

- Does your character have any specific prejudices? What are they and how do they affect interactions with others?

- Does he / she have an overpowering addiction considered a weakness...or perhaps a strength?

- Do they have a latent ability (or repressed memory) that can be brought out in the story?

- Is your character being used as a pawn in a much bigger plot behind the scenes?

- What lie have they told that will soon catch up & expose them?

FATHER:

MOTHER:

SIBLINGS:

FRIENDS:

HABITS / MANNERISMS

INTERNAL / EXTERNAL CONFLICTS:

PERSONAL STORY ARC

CHARACTER HISTORY

NAME

NICKNAME

BOOK

Series

IMPORTANCE

INFLUENCE

STRENGTH

COORDINATION

INTELLIGENCE

WISDOM

STREETWISE

DIPLOMACY

CHARISMA

WILL

Race:

Age: Weight:

LAWFUL   CHAOTIC
GOOD   GOOD

N

LAWFUL   CHAOTIC
EVIL   EVIL

OCCUPATION:

PORTRAIT

Roll In Story:

Physical Description

Personality

Discerning Features

Unique Talents / Abilities:

Character TRIGGER Questions:

-Is your character considered normal and acceptable in this society? Why not?

- Does your character have any mannerisms, habits or desires considered taboo?

- What does your character do that causes others to feel uncomfortable?

- Does he / she have any special needs that have to be met (such as medication or therapy)?

- Does your character have an unknown connection to a famous / infamous person or group in history?

- Does your character have a deep secret that could change the course of events?

- What are your characters core beliefs ? Name three (3) principles they will not compromise.

- What is the greatest loss your character has experienced?

- What is your characters greatest fear? How does that affect the way they make decisions?

- What are your characters dreams? What we desire forms our decisions, so what does he / she want?

- Does your character have any specific prejudices? What are they and how do they affect interactions with others?

- Does he / she have an overpowering addiction considered a weakness...or perhaps a strength?

- Do they have a latent ability (or repressed memory) that can be brought out in the story?

- Is your character being used as a pawn in a much bigger plot behind the scenes?

- What lie have they told that will soon catch up & expose them?

FATHER:

MOTHER:

SIBLINGS:

FRIENDS:

HABITS / MANNERISMS

INTERNAL / EXTERNAL CONFLICTS:

PERSONAL STORY ARC

CHARACTER HISTORY

NAME _____   BOOK _____

NICKNAME _____   Series _____

IMPORTANCE			
INFLUENCE			
STRENGTH			
COORDINATION			
INTELLIGENCE			
WISDOM			
STREETWISE			
DIPLOMACY			
CHARISMA			
WILL			

Race: _____

Age: _____   Weight: _____

PORTRAIT

LAWFUL GOOD .... CHAOTIC GOOD

N

LAWFUL EVIL .... CHAOTIC EVIL

OCCUPATION: _____

Roll In Story:
_____
_____
_____
_____
_____
_____
_____
_____
_____

Physical Description
_____
_____
_____
_____

Personality
_____
_____
_____
_____
_____

Discerning Features
_____
_____
_____

Unique Talents / Abilities:
_____
_____
_____
_____

Character TRIGGER Questions:

-Is your character considered normal and acceptable in this society? Why not?

- Does your character have any mannerisms, habits or desires considered taboo?

- What does your character do that causes others to feel uncomfortable?

- Does he / she have any special needs that have to be met (such as medication or therapy)?

- Does your character have an unknown connection to a famous / infamous person or group in history?

- Does your character have a deep secret that could change the course of events?

- What are your characters core beliefs ? Name three (3) principles they will not compromise.

- What is the greatest loss your character has experienced?

- What is your characters greatest fear? How does that affect the way they make decisions?

- What are your characters dreams? What we desire forms our decisions, so what does he / she want?

- Does your character have any specific prejudices? What are they and how do they affect interactions with others?

- Does he / she have an overpowering addiction considered a weakness...or perhaps a strength?

- Do they have a latent ability (or repressed memory) that can be brought out in the story?

- Is your character being used as a pawn in a much bigger plot behind the scenes?

- What lie have they told that will soon catch up & expose them?

FATHER:

MOTHER:

SIBLINGS:

FRIENDS:

HABITS / MANNERISMS

INTERNAL / EXTERNAL CONFLICTS:

PERSONAL STORY ARC

CHARACTER HISTORY

NAME _____

NICKNAME _____

BOOK _____

Series _____

IMPORTANCE				
INFLUENCE				
STRENGTH				
COORDINATION				
INTELLIGENCE				
WISDOM				
STREETWISE				
DIPLOMACY				
CHARISMA				
WILL				

Race: _____

Age: _____   Weight: _____

LAWFUL GOOD   CHAOTIC GOOD

N

LAWFUL EVIL   CHAOTIC EVIL

OCCUPATION: _____

PORTRAIT

Roll In Story:

_____
_____
_____
_____
_____
_____
_____
_____
_____
_____
_____
_____
_____
_____
_____
_____

Personality

_____
_____
_____
_____
_____
_____
_____
_____
_____
_____

Physical Description

_____
_____
_____
_____
_____
_____

Discerning Features

_____
_____
_____
_____
_____
_____

Unique Talents / Abilities:

_____
_____
_____
_____
_____

Character TRIGGER Questions:

-Is your character considered normal and acceptable in this society? Why not?

- Does your character have any mannerisms, habits or desires considered taboo?

- What does your character do that causes others to feel uncomfortable?

- Does he / she have any special needs that have to be met (such as medication or therapy)?

- Does your character have an unknown connection to a famous / infamous person or group in history?

- Does your character have a deep secret that could change the course of events?

- What are your characters core beliefs ? Name three (3) principles they will not compromise.

- What is the greatest loss your character has experienced?

- What is your characters greatest fear? How does that affect the way they make decisions?

- What are your characters dreams? What we desire forms our decisions, so what does he / she want?

- Does your character have any specific prejudices? What are they and how do they affect interactions with others?

- Does he / she have an overpowering addiction considered a weakness...or perhaps a strength?

- Do they have a latent ability (or repressed memory) that can be brought out in the story?

- Is your character being used as a pawn in a much bigger plot behind the scenes?

- What lie have they told that will soon catch up & expose them?

FATHER:

MOTHER:

SIBLINGS:

FRIENDS:

HABITS / MANNERISMS

INTERNAL / EXTERNAL CONFLICTS:

PERSONAL STORY ARC

CHARACTER HISTORY

NAME _____

NICKNAME _____

BOOK _____

Series _____

IMPORTANCE				
INFLUENCE				
STRENGTH				
COORDINATION				
INTELLIGENCE				
WISDOM				
STREETWISE				
DIPLOMACY				
CHARISMA				
WILL				

Race:

Age:

Weight:

PORTRAIT

LAWFUL GOOD   CHAOTIC GOOD

N

LAWFUL EVIL   CHAOTIC EVIL

OCCUPATION:

Roll In Story:

Physical Description

Personality

Discerning Features

Unique Talents / Abilities:

Character TRIGGER Questions:

- Is your character considered normal and acceptable in this society? Why not?
- Does your character have any mannerisms, habits or desires considered taboo?
- What does your character do that causes others to feel uncomfortable?
- Does he / she have any special needs that have to be met (such as medication or therapy)?
- Does your character have an unknown connection to a famous / infamous person or group in history?
- Does your character have a deep secret that could change the course of events?
- What are your characters core beliefs ? Name three (3) principles they will not compromise.

- What is the greatest loss your character has experienced?
- What is your characters greatest fear? How does that affect the way they make decisions?
- What are your characters dreams? What we desire forms our decisions, so what does he / she want?
- Does your character have any specific prejudices? What are they and how do they affect interactions with others?
- Does he / she have an overpowering addiction considered a weakness...or perhaps a strength?
- Do they have a latent ability (or repressed memory) that can be brought out in the story?
- Is your character being used as a pawn in a much bigger plot behind the scenes?
- What lie have they told that will soon catch up & expose them?

FATHER:

MOTHER:

SIBLINGS:

FRIENDS:

HABITS / MANNERISMS

INTERNAL / EXTERNAL CONFLICTS:

PERSONAL STORY ARC

CHARACTER HISTORY

NAME _____

BOOK _____

NICKNAME _____

Series _____

IMPORTANCE			
INFLUENCE			
STRENGTH			
COORDINATION			
INTELLIGENCE			
WISDOM			
STREETWISE			
DIPLOMACY			
CHARISMA			
WILL			

Race: _____

Age: _____ **Weight:** _____

LAWFUL GOOD   CHAOTIC GOOD

N

LAWFUL EVIL   CHAOTIC EVIL

OCCUPATION: _____

PORTRAIT

Roll In Story:

_____
_____
_____
_____
_____
_____
_____
_____
_____
_____
_____

Physical Description

_____
_____
_____
_____
_____
_____
_____

Personality

_____
_____
_____
_____
_____
_____

Discerning Features

_____
_____
_____
_____

Unique Talents / Abilities:

_____
_____
_____
_____
_____

Character TRIGGER Questions:

-Is your character considered normal and acceptable in this society? Why not?
- Does your character have any mannerisms, habits or desires considered taboo?
- What does your character do that causes others to feel uncomfortable?
- Does he / she have any special needs that have to be met (such as medication or therapy)?
- Does your character have an unknown connection to a famous / infamous person or group in history?
- Does your character have a deep secret that could change the course of events?
- What are your characters core beliefs ? Name three (3) principles they will not compromise.

- What is the greatest loss your character has experienced?
- What is your characters greatest fear? How does that affect the way they make decisions?
- What are your characters dreams? What we desire forms our decisions, so what does he / she want?
- Does your character have any specific prejudices? What are they and how do they affect interactions with others?
- Does he / she have an overpowering addiction considered a weakness...or perhaps a strength?
- Do they have a latent ability (or repressed memory) that can be brought out in the story?
- Is your character being used as a pawn in a much bigger plot behind the scenes?
- What lie have they told that will soon catch up & expose them?

FATHER:

MOTHER:

SIBLINGS:

FRIENDS:

HABITS / MANNERISMS

INTERNAL / EXTERNAL CONFLICTS:

PERSONAL STORY ARC

CHARACTER HISTORY

NAME _____

NICKNAME _____

BOOK _____

Series _____

IMPORTANCE				
INFLUENCE				
STRENGTH				
COORDINATION				
INTELLIGENCE				
WISDOM				
STREETWISE				
DIPLOMACY				
CHARISMA				
WILL				

Race: _____

Age: _____   Weight: _____

LAWFUL GOOD   CHAOTIC GOOD

N

LAWFUL EVIL   CHAOTIC EVIL

OCCUPATION:

PORTRAIT

Roll In Story:

_____
_____
_____
_____
_____
_____
_____
_____
_____
_____
_____
_____

Physical Description

_____
_____
_____
_____
_____
_____
_____

Personality

_____
_____
_____
_____
_____
_____

Discerning Features

_____
_____
_____

Unique Talents / Abilities:

_____
_____
_____
_____

Character TRIGGER Questions:

-Is your character considered normal and acceptable in this society? Why not?

- Does your character have any mannerisms, habits or desires considered taboo?

- What does your character do that causes others to feel uncomfortable?

- Does he / she have any special needs that have to be met (such as medication or therapy)?

- Does your character have an unknown connection to a famous / infamous person or group in history?

- Does your character have a deep secret that could change the course of events?

- What are your characters core beliefs ? Name three (3) principles they will not compromise.

- What is the greatest loss your character has experienced?

- What is your characters greatest fear? How does that affect the way they make decisions?

- What are your characters dreams? What we desire forms our decisions, so what does he / she want?

- Does your character have any specific prejudices? What are they and how do they affect interactions with others?

- Does he / she have an overpowering addiction considered a weakness...or perhaps a strength?

- Do they have a latent ability (or repressed memory) that can be brought out in the story?

- Is your character being used as a pawn in a much bigger plot behind the scenes?

- What lie have they told that will soon catch up & expose them?

FATHER:

MOTHER:

SIBLINGS:

FRIENDS:

HABITS / MANNERISMS

INTERNAL / EXTERNAL CONFLICTS:

PERSONAL STORY ARC

CHARACTER HISTORY

NAME _____

NICKNAME _____

BOOK _____

Series _____

IMPORTANCE			
INFLUENCE			
STRENGTH			
COORDINATION			
INTELLIGENCE			
WISDOM			
STREETWISE			
DIPLOMACY			
CHARISMA			
WILL			

Race: _____

Age: _____ Weight: _____

PORTRAIT

LAWFUL GOOD   CHAOTIC GOOD

N

LAWFUL EVIL   CHAOTIC EVIL

OCCUPATION: _____

Roll In Story:
_____
_____
_____
_____
_____
_____
_____
_____
_____
_____
_____
_____

Physical Description
_____
_____
_____
_____
_____
_____

Personality
_____
_____
_____
_____
_____
_____

Discerning Features
_____
_____
_____
_____

Unique Talents / Abilities:
_____
_____
_____
_____
_____
_____

Character TRIGGER Questions:

-Is your character considered normal and acceptable in this society? Why not?

- Does your character have any mannerisms, habits or desires considered taboo?

- What does your character do that causes others to feel uncomfortable?

- Does he / she have any special needs that have to be met (such as medication or therapy)?

- Does your character have an unknown connection to a famous / infamous person or group in history?

- Does your character have a deep secret that could change the course of events?

- What are your characters core beliefs ? Name three (3) principles they will not compromise.

- What is the greatest loss your character has experienced?

- What is your characters greatest fear? How does that affect the way they make decisions?

- What are your characters dreams? What we desire forms our decisions, so what does he / she want?

- Does your character have any specific prejudices? What are they and how do they affect interactions with others?

- Does he / she have an overpowering addiction considered a weakness...or perhaps a strength?

- Do they have a latent ability (or repressed memory) that can be brought out in the story?

- Is your character being used as a pawn in a much bigger plot behind the scenes?

- What lie have they told that will soon catch up & expose them?

FATHER:

MOTHER:

SIBLINGS:

FRIENDS:

HABITS / MANNERISMS

INTERNAL / EXTERNAL CONFLICTS:

PERSONAL STORY ARC

CHARACTER HISTORY

NAME _____

NICKNAME _____

BOOK _____

Series _____

IMPORTANCE					
INFLUENCE					
STRENGTH					
COORDINATION					
INTELLIGENCE					
WISDOM					
STREETWISE					
DIPLOMACY					
CHARISMA					
WILL					

Race: _____

Age: _____   Weight: _____

LAWFUL GOOD   CHAOTIC GOOD

N

LAWFUL EVIL   CHAOTIC EVIL

OCCUPATION: _____

PORTRAIT

Roll In Story:

_____
_____
_____
_____
_____
_____
_____
_____
_____
_____
_____

Physical Description

_____
_____
_____
_____

Discerning Features

_____
_____
_____
_____

Personality

_____
_____
_____
_____
_____

Unique Talents / Abilities:

_____
_____
_____
_____

Character TRIGGER Questions:

- Is your character considered normal and acceptable in this society? Why not?
- Does your character have any mannerisms, habits or desires considered taboo?
- What does your character do that causes others to feel uncomfortable?
- Does he / she have any special needs that have to be met (such as medication or therapy)?
- Does your character have an unknown connection to a famous / infamous person or group in history?
- Does your character have a deep secret that could change the course of events?
- What are your characters core beliefs ? Name three (3) principles they will not compromise.

- What is the greatest loss your character has experienced?
- What is your characters greatest fear? How does that affect the way they make decisions?
- What are your characters dreams? What we desire forms our decisions, so what does he / she want?
- Does your character have any specific prejudices? What are they and how do they affect interactions with others?
- Does he / she have an overpowering addiction considered a weakness...or perhaps a strength?
- Do they have a latent ability (or repressed memory) that can be brought out in the story?
- Is your character being used as a pawn in a much bigger plot behind the scenes?
- What lie have they told that will soon catch up & expose them?

FATHER:

MOTHER:

SIBLINGS:

FRIENDS:

HABITS / MANNERISMS

INTERNAL / EXTERNAL CONFLICTS:

PERSONAL STORY ARC

CHARACTER HISTORY

NAME _____

NICKNAME _____

BOOK _____

Series _____

IMPORTANCE	
INFLUENCE	
STRENGTH	
COORDINATION	
INTELLIGENCE	
WISDOM	
STREETWISE	
DIPLOMACY	
CHARISMA	
WILL	

Race: _____

Age: _____ Weight: _____

LAWFUL GOOD ... CHAOTIC GOOD

N

LAWFUL EVIL ... CHAOTIC EVIL

OCCUPATION: _____

PORTRAIT

Roll In Story:
_____
_____
_____
_____
_____
_____
_____
_____
_____
_____
_____
_____

Physical Description
_____
_____
_____
_____
_____

Personality
_____
_____
_____
_____
_____
_____
_____
_____
_____

Discerning Features
_____
_____
_____
_____

Unique Talents / Abilities:
_____
_____
_____
_____
_____

Character TRIGGER Questions:

-Is your character considered normal and acceptable in this society? Why not?

- Does your character have any mannerisms, habits or desires considered taboo?

- What does your character do that causes others to feel uncomfortable?

- Does he / she have any special needs that have to be met (such as medication or therapy)?

- Does your character have an unknown connection to a famous / infamous person or group in history?

- Does your character have a deep secret that could change the course of events?

- What are your characters core beliefs? Name three (3) principles they will not compromise.

- What is the greatest loss your character has experienced?

- What is your characters greatest fear? How does that affect the way they make decisions?

- What are your characters dreams? What we desire forms our decisions, so what does he / she want?

- Does your character have any specific prejudices? What are they and how do they affect interactions with others?

- Does he / she have an overpowering addiction considered a weakness...or perhaps a strength?

- Do they have a latent ability (or repressed memory) that can be brought out in the story?

- Is your character being used as a pawn in a much bigger plot behind the scenes?

- What lie have they told that will soon catch up & expose them?

FATHER:

MOTHER:

SIBLINGS:

FRIENDS:

HABITS / MANNERISMS

INTERNAL / EXTERNAL CONFLICTS:

PERSONAL STORY ARC

CHARACTER HISTORY

NAME _____

NICKNAME _____

BOOK _____

Series _____

IMPORTANCE				
INFLUENCE				
STRENGTH				
COORDINATION				
INTELLIGENCE				
WISDOM				
STREETWISE				
DIPLOMACY				
CHARISMA				
WILL				

Race: _____

Age: _____ Weight: _____

PORTRAIT

LAWFUL GOOD   CHAOTIC GOOD

N

LAWFUL EVIL   CHAOTIC EVIL

OCCUPATION: _____

Roll In Story:
_____
_____
_____
_____
_____
_____
_____
_____
_____
_____
_____
_____

Physical Description
_____
_____
_____
_____
_____

Personality
_____
_____
_____
_____
_____
_____
_____
_____

Discerning Features
_____
_____
_____

Unique Talents / Abilities:
_____
_____
_____
_____
_____

Character TRIGGER Questions:

- Is your character considered normal and acceptable in this society? Why not?
- Does your character have any mannerisms, habits or desires considered taboo?
- What does your character do that causes others to feel uncomfortable?
- Does he / she have any special needs that have to be met (such as medication or therapy)?
- Does your character have an unknown connection to a famous / infamous person or group in history?
- Does your character have a deep secret that could change the course of events?
- What are your characters core beliefs ? Name three (3) principles they will not compromise.

- What is the greatest loss your character has experienced?
- What is your characters greatest fear? How does that affect the way they make decisions?
- What are your characters dreams? What we desire forms our decisions, so what does he / she want?
- Does your character have any specific prejudices? What are they and how do they affect interactions with others?
- Does he / she have an overpowering addiction considered a weakness...or perhaps a strength?
- Do they have a latent ability (or repressed memory) that can be brought out in the story?
- Is your character being used as a pawn in a much bigger plot behind the scenes?
- What lie have they told that will soon catch up & expose them?

FATHER:

MOTHER:

SIBLINGS:

FRIENDS:

HABITS / MANNERISMS

INTERNAL / EXTERNAL CONFLICTS:

PERSONAL STORY ARC

CHARACTER HISTORY

NAME _____

NICKNAME _____

BOOK _____

Series _____

IMPORTANCE				
INFLUENCE				
STRENGTH				
COORDINATION				
INTELLIGENCE				
WISDOM				
STREETWISE				
DIPLOMACY				
CHARISMA				
WILL				

Race: _____

Age: _____ Weight: _____

LAWFUL GOOD   CHAOTIC GOOD

N

LAWFUL EVIL   CHAOTIC EVIL

OCCUPATION: _____

PORTRAIT

Roll In Story:

_____
_____
_____
_____
_____
_____
_____
_____
_____
_____
_____
_____
_____

Physical Description

_____
_____
_____
_____
_____

Personality

_____
_____
_____
_____
_____
_____
_____
_____
_____
_____
_____

Discerning Features

_____
_____
_____
_____
_____

Unique Talents / Abilities:

_____
_____
_____
_____
_____

Character TRIGGER Questions:

-Is your character considered normal and acceptable in this society? Why not?

- Does your character have any mannerisms, habits or desires considered taboo?

- What does your character do that causes others to feel uncomfortable?

- Does he / she have any special needs that have to be met (such as medication or therapy)?

- Does your character have an unknown connection to a famous / infamous person or group in history?

- Does your character have a deep secret that could change the course of events?

- What are your characters core beliefs ? Name three (3) principles they will not compromise.

- What is the greatest loss your character has experienced?

- What is your characters greatest fear? How does that affect the way they make decisions?

- What are your characters dreams? What we desire forms our decisions, so what does he / she want?

- Does your character have any specific prejudices? What are they and how do they affect interactions with others?

- Does he / she have an overpowering addiction considered a weakness...or perhaps a strength?

- Do they have a latent ability (or repressed memory) that can be brought out in the story?

- Is your character being used as a pawn in a much bigger plot behind the scenes?

- What lie have they told that will soon catch up & expose them?

FATHER:

MOTHER:

SIBLINGS:

FRIENDS:

HABITS / MANNERISMS

INTERNAL / EXTERNAL CONFLICTS:

PERSONAL STORY ARC

CHARACTER HISTORY

NAME _____

NICKNAME _____

BOOK _____

Series _____

IMPORTANCE
INFLUENCE

STRENGTH
COORDINATION

INTELLIGENCE
WISDOM
STREETWISE
DIPLOMACY
CHARISMA
WILL

Race: _____

Age: _____   Weight: _____

PORTRAIT

LAWFUL
GOOD

CHAOTIC
GOOD

N

LAWFUL
EVIL

CHAOTIC
EVIL

OCCUPATION:

Roll In Story:

_____
_____
_____
_____
_____
_____
_____
_____
_____
_____
_____
_____
_____

Physical Description

_____
_____
_____
_____
_____

Personality

_____
_____
_____
_____
_____
_____
_____

Discerning Features

_____
_____
_____
_____

Unique Talents / Abilities:

_____
_____
_____
_____
_____

Character TRIGGER Questions:

-Is your character considered normal and acceptable in this society? Why not?
- Does your character have any mannerisms, habits or desires considered taboo?
- What does your character do that causes others to feel uncomfortable?
- Does he / she have any special needs that have to be met (such as medication or therapy)?
- Does your character have an unknown connection to a famous / infamous person or group in history?
- Does your character have a deep secret that could change the course of events?
- What are your characters core beliefs ? Name three (3) principles they will not compromise.

- What is the greatest loss your character has experienced?
- What is your characters greatest fear? How does that affect the way they make decisions?
- What are your characters dreams? What we desire forms our decisions, so what does he / she want?
- Does your character have any specific prejudices? What are they and how do they affect interactions with others?
- Does he / she have an overpowering addiction considered a weakness...or perhaps a strength?
- Do they have a latent ability (or repressed memory) that can be brought out in the story?
- Is your character being used as a pawn in a much bigger plot behind the scenes?
- What lie have they told that will soon catch up & expose them?

FATHER:

MOTHER:

SIBLINGS:

FRIENDS:

HABITS / MANNERISMS

INTERNAL / EXTERNAL CONFLICTS:

PERSONAL STORY ARC

CHARACTER HISTORY

NAME _____

NICKNAME _____

BOOK _____

Series _____

IMPORTANCE				
INFLUENCE				
STRENGTH				
COORDINATION				
INTELLIGENCE				
WISDOM				
STREETWISE				
DIPLOMACY				
CHARISMA				
WILL				

Race: _____

Age: _____   Weight: _____

LAWFUL GOOD   CHAOTIC GOOD

N

LAWFUL EVIL   CHAOTIC EVIL

OCCUPATION: _____

PORTRAIT

Roll In Story:
_____
_____
_____
_____
_____
_____
_____
_____
_____
_____
_____
_____

Physical Description
_____
_____
_____
_____
_____

Personality
_____
_____
_____
_____
_____
_____
_____

Discerning Features
_____
_____
_____
_____

Unique Talents / Abilities:
_____
_____
_____
_____
_____

Character TRIGGER Questions:

- Is your character considered normal and acceptable in this society? Why not?
- Does your character have any mannerisms, habits or desires considered taboo?
- What does your character do that causes others to feel uncomfortable?
- Does he / she have any special needs that have to be met (such as medication or therapy)?
- Does your character have an unknown connection to a famous / infamous person or group in history?
- Does your character have a deep secret that could change the course of events?
- What are your characters core beliefs? Name three (3) principles they will not compromise.

- What is the greatest loss your character has experienced?
- What is your characters greatest fear? How does that affect the way they make decisions?
- What are your characters dreams? What we desire forms our decisions, so what does he / she want?
- Does your character have any specific prejudices? What are they and how do they affect interactions with others?
- Does he / she have an overpowering addiction considered a weakness...or perhaps a strength?
- Do they have a latent ability (or repressed memory) that can be brought out in the story?
- Is your character being used as a pawn in a much bigger plot behind the scenes?
- What lie have they told that will soon catch up & expose them?

FATHER:

MOTHER:

SIBLINGS:

FRIENDS:

HABITS / MANNERISMS

INTERNAL / EXTERNAL CONFLICTS:

PERSONAL STORY ARC

CHARACTER HISTORY

NAME _____ BOOK _____

NICKNAME _____ Series _____

IMPORTANCE [ ][ ][ ][ ]
INFLUENCE [ ][ ][ ][ ]

STRENGTH [ ]
COORDINATION [ ]

INTELLIGENCE [ ]
WISDOM [ ]
STREETWISE [ ]
DIPLOMACY [ ]
CHARISMA [ ]
WILL [ ]

Race: _____

Age: _____ Weight: _____

PORTRAIT

LAWFUL
GOOD

CHAOTIC
GOOD

N

LAWFUL
EVIL

CHAOTIC
EVIL

OCCUPATION:

Roll In Story:
_____
_____
_____
_____
_____
_____
_____
_____
_____
_____
_____
_____
_____

Physical Description
_____
_____
_____
_____
_____
_____

Personality
_____
_____
_____
_____
_____
_____
_____
_____
_____

Discerning Features
_____
_____
_____

Unique Talents / Abilities:
_____
_____
_____
_____
_____

Character TRIGGER Questions:

- Is your character considered normal and acceptable in this society? Why not?
- Does your character have any mannerisms, habits or desires considered taboo?
- What does your character do that causes others to feel uncomfortable?
- Does he / she have any special needs that have to be met (such as medication or therapy)?
- Does your character have an unknown connection to a famous / infamous person or group in history?
- Does your character have a deep secret that could change the course of events?
- What are your characters core beliefs ? Name three (3) principles they will not compromise.

- What is the greatest loss your character has experienced?
- What is your characters greatest fear? How does that affect the way they make decisions?
- What are your characters dreams? What we desire forms our decisions, so what does he / she want?
- Does your character have any specific prejudices? What are they and how do they affect interactions with others?
- Does he / she have an overpowering addiction considered a weakness...or perhaps a strength?
- Do they have a latent ability (or repressed memory) that can be brought out in the story?
- Is your character being used as a pawn in a much bigger plot behind the scenes?
- What lie have they told that will soon catch up & expose them?

FATHER:

MOTHER:

SIBLINGS:

FRIENDS:

HABITS / MANNERISMS

INTERNAL / EXTERNAL CONFLICTS:

PERSONAL STORY ARC

CHARACTER HISTORY

NAME _____

NICKNAME _____

BOOK _____

Series _____

IMPORTANCE	
INFLUENCE	
STRENGTH	
COORDINATION	
INTELLIGENCE	
WISDOM	
STREETWISE	
DIPLOMACY	
CHARISMA	
WILL	

Race: _____

Age: _____   Weight: _____

LAWFUL GOOD   CHAOTIC GOOD

N

LAWFUL EVIL   CHAOTIC EVIL

OCCUPATION: _____

PORTRAIT

Roll In Story:
_____
_____
_____
_____
_____
_____
_____
_____
_____
_____
_____

Physical Description
_____
_____
_____
_____

Personality
_____
_____
_____
_____
_____

Discerning Features
_____
_____
_____

Unique Talents / Abilities:
_____
_____
_____
_____

Character TRIGGER Questions:

- Is your character considered normal and acceptable in this society? Why not?
- Does your character have any mannerisms, habits or desires considered taboo?
- What does your character do that causes others to feel uncomfortable?
- Does he / she have any special needs that have to be met (such as medication or therapy)?
- Does your character have an unknown connection to a famous / infamous person or group in history?
- Does your character have a deep secret that could change the course of events?
- What are your characters core beliefs ? Name three (3) principles they will not compromise.

- What is the greatest loss your character has experienced?
- What is your characters greatest fear? How does that affect the way they make decisions?
- What are your characters dreams? What we desire forms our decisions, so what does he / she want?
- Does your character have any specific prejudices? What are they and how do they affect interactions with others?
- Does he / she have an overpowering addiction considered a weakness...or perhaps a strength?
- Do they have a latent ability (or repressed memory) that can be brought out in the story?
- Is your character being used as a pawn in a much bigger plot behind the scenes?
- What lie have they told that will soon catch up & expose them?

FATHER:

MOTHER:

SIBLINGS:

FRIENDS:

HABITS / MANNERISMS

INTERNAL / EXTERNAL CONFLICTS:

PERSONAL STORY ARC

CHARACTER HISTORY

NAME _____

NICKNAME _____

BOOK _____

Series _____

IMPORTANCE				
INFLUENCE				
STRENGTH				
COORDINATION				
INTELLIGENCE				
WISDOM				
STREETWISE				
DIPLOMACY				
CHARISMA				
WILL				

Race: _____

Age: _____   Weight: _____

PORTRAIT

LAWFUL GOOD .... CHAOTIC GOOD

N

LAWFUL EVIL .... CHAOTIC EVIL

OCCUPATION: _____

Roll In Story:

_____

Personality

_____

Physical Description

_____

Discerning Features

_____

Unique Talents / Abilities:

_____

Character TRIGGER Questions:

-Is your character considered normal and acceptable in this society? Why not?

- Does your character have any mannerisms, habits or desires considered taboo?

- What does your character do that causes others to feel uncomfortable?

- Does he / she have any special needs that have to be met (such as medication or therapy)?

- Does your character have an unknown connection to a famous / infamous person or group in history?

- Does your character have a deep secret that could change the course of events?

- What are your characters core beliefs ? Name three (3) principles they will not compromise.

- What is the greatest loss your character has experienced?

- What is your characters greatest fear? How does that affect the way they make decisions?

- What are your characters dreams? What we desire forms our decisions, so what does he / she want?

- Does your character have any specific prejudices? What are they and how do they affect interactions with others?

- Does he / she have an overpowering addiction considered a weakness...or perhaps a strength?

- Do they have a latent ability (or repressed memory) that can be brought out in the story?

- Is your character being used as a pawn in a much bigger plot behind the scenes?

- What lie have they told that will soon catch up & expose them?

FATHER:

MOTHER:

SIBLINGS:

FRIENDS:

HABITS / MANNERISMS

INTERNAL / EXTERNAL CONFLICTS:

PERSONAL STORY ARC

CHARACTER HISTORY

NAME _____ BOOK _____

NICKNAME _____ Series _____

IMPORTANCE _____
INFLUENCE _____

STRENGTH _____
COORDINATION _____

INTELLIGENCE _____
WISDOM _____
STREETWISE _____
DIPLOMACY _____
CHARISMA _____
WILL _____

Race: _____

Age: _____ Weight: _____

PORTRAIT

LAWFUL GOOD   CHAOTIC GOOD

N

LAWFUL EVIL   CHAOTIC EVIL

OCCUPATION:

Roll In Story:
_____
_____
_____
_____
_____
_____
_____
_____
_____
_____

Physical Description
_____
_____
_____
_____
_____
_____

Personality
_____
_____
_____
_____
_____
_____
_____

Discerning Features
_____
_____
_____
_____

Unique Talents / Abilities:
_____
_____
_____
_____
_____

Character TRIGGER Questions:

-Is your character considered normal and acceptable in this society? Why not?
- Does your character have any mannerisms, habits or desires considered taboo?
- What does your character do that causes others to feel uncomfortable?
- Does he / she have any special needs that have to be met (such as medication or therapy)?
- Does your character have an unknown connection to a famous / infamous person or group in history?
- Does your character have a deep secret that could change the course of events?
- What are your characters core beliefs ? Name three (3) principles they will not compromise.

- What is the greatest loss your character has experienced?
- What is your characters greatest fear? How does that affect the way they make decisions?
- What are your characters dreams? What we desire forms our decisions, so what does he / she want?
- Does your character have any specific prejudices? What are they and how do they affect interactions with others?
- Does he / she have an overpowering addiction considered a weakness...or perhaps a strength?
- Do they have a latent ability (or repressed memory) that can be brought out in the story?
- Is your character being used as a pawn in a much bigger plot behind the scenes?
- What lie have they told that will soon catch up & expose them?

FATHER:

MOTHER:

SIBLINGS:

FRIENDS:

HABITS / MANNERISMS

INTERNAL / EXTERNAL CONFLICTS:

PERSONAL STORY ARC

CHARACTER HISTORY

NAME _____

NICKNAME _____

BOOK

Series

IMPORTANCE
INFLUENCE

STRENGTH
COORDINATION

INTELLIGENCE
WISDOM
STREETWISE
DIPLOMACY
CHARISMA
WILL

Race: _____

Age: _____   Weight: _____

PORTRAIT

LAWFUL
GOOD

CHAOTIC
GOOD

N

Roll In Story:
_____
_____
_____
_____
_____
_____
_____
_____
_____
_____
_____
_____
_____

LAWFUL
EVIL

CHAOTIC
EVIL

OCCUPATION:

Physical Description
_____
_____
_____
_____
_____

Personality
_____
_____
_____
_____
_____
_____
_____
_____

Discerning Features
_____
_____
_____
_____
_____

Unique Talents / Abilities:
_____
_____
_____
_____
_____
_____

Character TRIGGER Questions:

-Is your character considered normal and acceptable in this society? Why not?

- Does your character have any mannerisms, habits or desires considered taboo?

- What does your character do that causes others to feel uncomfortable?

- Does he / she have any special needs that have to be met (such as medication or therapy)?

- Does your character have an unknown connection to a famous / infamous person or group in history?

- Does your character have a deep secret that could change the course of events?

- What are your characters core beliefs ? Name three (3) principles they will not compromise.

- What is the greatest loss your character has experienced?

- What is your characters greatest fear? How does that affect the way they make decisions?

- What are your characters dreams? What we desire forms our decisions, so what does he / she want?

- Does your character have any specific prejudices? What are they and how do they affect interactions with others?

- Does he / she have an overpowering addiction considered a weakness...or perhaps a strength?

- Do they have a latent ability (or repressed memory) that can be brought out in the story?

- Is your character being used as a pawn in a much bigger plot behind the scenes?

- What lie have they told that will soon catch up & expose them?

FATHER:

MOTHER:

SIBLINGS:

FRIENDS:

HABITS / MANNERISMS

INTERNAL / EXTERNAL CONFLICTS:

PERSONAL STORY ARC

CHARACTER HISTORY

NAME _____

NICKNAME _____

BOOK _____

Series _____

IMPORTANCE	
INFLUENCE	
STRENGTH	
COORDINATION	
INTELLIGENCE	
WISDOM	
STREETWISE	
DIPLOMACY	
CHARISMA	
WILL	

Race: _____

Age: _____ Weight: _____

PORTRAIT

LAWFUL GOOD   CHAOTIC GOOD

N

LAWFUL EVIL   CHAOTIC EVIL

OCCUPATION:

Roll In Story:

Physical Description

Personality

Discerning Features

Unique Talents / Abilities:

Character TRIGGER Questions:

- Is your character considered normal and acceptable in this society? Why not?
- Does your character have any mannerisms, habits or desires considered taboo?
- What does your character do that causes others to feel uncomfortable?
- Does he / she have any special needs that have to be met (such as medication or therapy)?
- Does your character have an unknown connection to a famous / infamous person or group in history?
- Does your character have a deep secret that could change the course of events?
- What are your characters core beliefs ? Name three (3) principles they will not compromise.

- What is the greatest loss your character has experienced?
- What is your characters greatest fear? How does that affect the way they make decisions?
- What are your characters dreams? What we desire forms our decisions, so what does he / she want?
- Does your character have any specific prejudices? What are they and how do they affect interactions with others?
- Does he / she have an overpowering addiction considered a weakness...or perhaps a strength?
- Do they have a latent ability (or repressed memory) that can be brought out in the story?
- Is your character being used as a pawn in a much bigger plot behind the scenes?
- What lie have they told that will soon catch up & expose them?

FATHER:

MOTHER:

SIBLINGS:

FRIENDS:

HABITS / MANNERISMS

INTERNAL / EXTERNAL CONFLICTS:

PERSONAL STORY ARC

CHARACTER HISTORY

NAME

NICKNAME

BOOK

Series

IMPORTANCE				
INFLUENCE				
STRENGTH				
COORDINATION				
INTELLIGENCE				
WISDOM				
STREETWISE				
DIPLOMACY				
CHARISMA				
WILL				

Race:

Age:

Weight:

PORTRAIT

LAWFUL GOOD

CHAOTIC GOOD

N

LAWFUL EVIL

CHAOTIC EVIL

OCCUPATION:

Roll In Story:

Personality

Physical Description

Discerning Features

Unique Talents / Abilities:

Character TRIGGER Questions:

-Is your character considered normal and acceptable in this society? Why not?

- Does your character have any mannerisms, habits or desires considered taboo?

- What does your character do that causes others to feel uncomfortable?

- Does he / she have any special needs that have to be met (such as medication or therapy)?

- Does your character have an unknown connection to a famous / infamous person or group in history?

- Does your character have a deep secret that could change the course of events?

- What are your characters core beliefs ? Name three (3) principles they will not compromise.

- What is the greatest loss your character has experienced?

- What is your characters greatest fear? How does that affect the way they make decisions?

- What are your characters dreams? What we desire forms our decisions, so what does he / she want?

- Does your character have any specific prejudices? What are they and how do they affect interactions with others?

- Does he / she have an overpowering addiction considered a weakness...or perhaps a strength?

- Do they have a latent ability (or repressed memory) that can be brought out in the story?

- Is your character being used as a pawn in a much bigger plot behind the scenes?

- What lie have they told that will soon catch up & expose them?

FATHER:

MOTHER:

SIBLINGS:

FRIENDS:

HABITS / MANNERISMS

INTERNAL / EXTERNAL CONFLICTS:

PERSONAL STORY ARC

CHARACTER HISTORY

NAME

NICKNAME

BOOK

Series

IMPORTANCE

INFLUENCE

STRENGTH

COORDINATION

INTELLIGENCE

WISDOM

STREETWISE

DIPLOMACY

CHARISMA

WILL

Race:

Age:

Weight:

LAWFUL
GOOD

CHAOTIC
GOOD

N

LAWFUL
EVIL

CHAOTIC
EVIL

PORTRAIT

Roll In Story:

OCCUPATION:

Physical Description

Personality

Discerning Features

Unique Talents / Abilities:

Character TRIGGER Questions:

- Is your character considered normal and acceptable in this society? Why not?
- Does your character have any mannerisms, habits or desires considered taboo?
- What does your character do that causes others to feel uncomfortable?
- Does he / she have any special needs that have to be met (such as medication or therapy)?
- Does your character have an unknown connection to a famous / infamous person or group in history?
- Does your character have a deep secret that could change the course of events?
- What are your characters core beliefs ? Name three (3) principles they will not compromise.

- What is the greatest loss your character has experienced?
- What is your characters greatest fear? How does that affect the way they make decisions?
- What are your characters dreams? What we desire forms our decisions, so what does he / she want?
- Does your character have any specific prejudices? What are they and how do they affect interactions with others?
- Does he / she have an overpowering addiction considered a weakness...or perhaps a strength?
- Do they have a latent ability (or repressed memory) that can be brought out in the story?
- Is your character being used as a pawn in a much bigger plot behind the scenes?
- What lie have they told that will soon catch up & expose them?

FATHER:

MOTHER:

SIBLINGS:

FRIENDS:

HABITS / MANNERISMS

INTERNAL / EXTERNAL CONFLICTS:

PERSONAL STORY ARC

CHARACTER HISTORY

NAME _____

NICKNAME _____

BOOK _____

Series _____

IMPORTANCE				
INFLUENCE				
STRENGTH				
COORDINATION				
INTELLIGENCE				
WISDOM				
STREETWISE				
DIPLOMACY				
CHARISMA				
WILL				

Race: _____

Age: _____ Weight: _____

LAWFUL GOOD   CHAOTIC GOOD

N

LAWFUL EVIL   CHAOTIC EVIL

OCCUPATION: _____

PORTRAIT

Roll In Story:

_____
_____
_____
_____
_____
_____
_____
_____
_____
_____
_____
_____

Personality

_____
_____
_____
_____
_____
_____
_____

Physical Description

_____
_____
_____
_____
_____

Discerning Features

_____
_____
_____
_____

Unique Talents / Abilities:

_____
_____
_____
_____

Character TRIGGER Questions:

-Is your character considered normal and acceptable in this society? Why not?
- Does your character have any mannerisms, habits or desires considered taboo?
- What does your character do that causes others to feel uncomfortable?
- Does he / she have any special needs that have to be met (such as medication or therapy)?
- Does your character have an unknown connection to a famous / infamous person or group in history?
- Does your character have a deep secret that could change the course of events?
- What are your characters core beliefs ? Name three (3) principles they will not compromise.

- What is the greatest loss your character has experienced?
- What is your characters greatest fear? How does that affect the way they make decisions?
- What are your characters dreams? What we desire forms our decisions, so what does he / she want?
- Does your character have any specific prejudices? What are they and how do they affect interactions with others?
- Does he / she have an overpowering addiction considered a weakness...or perhaps a strength?
- Do they have a latent ability (or repressed memory) that can be brought out in the story?
- Is your character being used as a pawn in a much bigger plot behind the scenes?
- What lie have they told that will soon catch up & expose them?

FATHER:

MOTHER:

SIBLINGS:

FRIENDS:

HABITS / MANNERISMS

INTERNAL / EXTERNAL CONFLICTS:

PERSONAL STORY ARC

CHARACTER HISTORY

NAME _____ BOOK _____

NICKNAME _____ Series _____

IMPORTANCE				
INFLUENCE				
STRENGTH				
COORDINATION				
INTELLIGENCE				
WISDOM				
STREETWISE				
DIPLOMACY				
CHARISMA				
WILL				

Race: _____

Age: _____ Weight: _____

PORTRAIT

LAWFUL GOOD   CHAOTIC GOOD

N

LAWFUL EVIL   CHAOTIC EVIL

OCCUPATION:

Roll In Story:

_____
_____
_____
_____
_____
_____
_____
_____
_____
_____
_____
_____

Physical Description

_____
_____
_____
_____
_____

Personality

_____
_____
_____
_____
_____
_____

Discerning Features

_____
_____
_____
_____

Unique Talents / Abilities:

_____
_____
_____
_____

Character TRIGGER Questions:

-Is your character considered normal and acceptable in this society? Why not?
- Does your character have any mannerisms, habits or desires considered taboo?
- What does your character do that causes others to feel uncomfortable?
- Does he / she have any special needs that have to be met (such as medication or therapy)?
- Does your character have an unknown connection to a famous / infamous person or group in history?
- Does your character have a deep secret that could change the course of events?
- What are your characters core beliefs ? Name three (3) principles they will not compromise.

- What is the greatest loss your character has experienced?
- What is your characters greatest fear? How does that affect the way they make decisions?
- What are your characters dreams? What we desire forms our decisions, so what does he / she want?
- Does your character have any specific prejudices? What are they and how do they affect interactions with others?
- Does he / she have an overpowering addiction considered a weakness...or perhaps a strength?
- Do they have a latent ability (or repressed memory) that can be brought out in the story?
- Is your character being used as a pawn in a much bigger plot behind the scenes?
- What lie have they told that will soon catch up & expose them?

FATHER:

MOTHER:

SIBLINGS:

FRIENDS:

HABITS / MANNERISMS

INTERNAL / EXTERNAL CONFLICTS:

PERSONAL STORY ARC

CHARACTER HISTORY

NAME

NICKNAME

BOOK

Series

IMPORTANCE

INFLUENCE

STRENGTH

COORDINATION

INTELLIGENCE

WISDOM

STREETWISE

DIPLOMACY

CHARISMA

WILL

Race:

Age:

Weight:

PORTRAIT

LAWFUL
GOOD

CHAOTIC
GOOD

N

LAWFUL
EVIL

CHAOTIC
EVIL

OCCUPATION:

Roll In Story:

Physical Description

Personality

Discerning Features

Unique Talents / Abilities:

Character TRIGGER Questions:

-Is your character considered normal and acceptable in this society? Why not?

- Does your character have any mannerisms, habits or desires considered taboo?

- What does your character do that causes others to feel uncomfortable?

- Does he / she have any special needs that have to be met (such as medication or therapy)?

- Does your character have an unknown connection to a famous / infamous person or group in history?

- Does your character have a deep secret that could change the course of events?

- What are your characters core beliefs ? Name three (3) principles they will not compromise.

- What is the greatest loss your character has experienced?

- What is your characters greatest fear? How does that affect the way they make decisions?

- What are your characters dreams? What we desire forms our decisions, so what does he / she want?

- Does your character have any specific prejudices? What are they and how do they affect interactions with others?

- Does he / she have an overpowering addiction considered a weakness...or perhaps a strength?

- Do they have a latent ability (or repressed memory) that can be brought out in the story?

- Is your character being used as a pawn in a much bigger plot behind the scenes?

- What lie have they told that will soon catch up & expose them?

FATHER:

MOTHER:

SIBLINGS:

FRIENDS:

HABITS / MANNERISMS

INTERNAL / EXTERNAL CONFLICTS:

PERSONAL STORY ARC

CHARACTER HISTORY

NAME _____   BOOK _____

NICKNAME _____   Series _____

IMPORTANCE				
INFLUENCE				
STRENGTH				
COORDINATION				
INTELLIGENCE				
WISDOM				
STREETWISE				
DIPLOMACY				
CHARISMA				
WILL				

Race: _____

Age: _____   Weight: _____

PORTRAIT

LAWFUL GOOD   CHAOTIC GOOD

N

LAWFUL EVIL   CHAOTIC EVIL

OCCUPATION:

Roll In Story:

_____
_____
_____
_____
_____
_____
_____
_____
_____
_____
_____
_____
_____

Physical Description

_____
_____
_____
_____

Personality

_____
_____
_____
_____
_____
_____
_____

Discerning Features

_____
_____
_____
_____

Unique Talents / Abilities:

_____
_____
_____
_____

Character TRIGGER Questions:

- Is your character considered normal and acceptable in this society? Why not?
- Does your character have any mannerisms, habits or desires considered taboo?
- What does your character do that causes others to feel uncomfortable?
- Does he / she have any special needs that have to be met (such as medication or therapy)?
- Does your character have an unknown connection to a famous / infamous person or group in history?
- Does your character have a deep secret that could change the course of events?
- What are your characters core beliefs ? Name three (3) principles they will not compromise.

- What is the greatest loss your character has experienced?
- What is your characters greatest fear? How does that affect the way they make decisions?
- What are your characters dreams? What we desire forms our decisions, so what does he / she want?
- Does your character have any specific prejudices? What are they and how do they affect interactions with others?
- Does he / she have an overpowering addiction considered a weakness...or perhaps a strength?
- Do they have a latent ability (or repressed memory) that can be brought out in the story?
- Is your character being used as a pawn in a much bigger plot behind the scenes?
- What lie have they told that will soon catch up & expose them?

FATHER:

MOTHER:

SIBLINGS:

FRIENDS:

HABITS / MANNERISMS

INTERNAL / EXTERNAL CONFLICTS:

PERSONAL STORY ARC

CHARACTER HISTORY

NAME

NICKNAME

BOOK

Series

IMPORTANCE

INFLUENCE

STRENGTH

COORDINATION

INTELLIGENCE

WISDOM

STREETWISE

DIPLOMACY

CHARISMA

WILL

Race:

Age:

Weight:

LAWFUL
GOOD

CHAOTIC
GOOD

N

LAWFUL
EVIL

CHAOTIC
EVIL

PORTRAIT

Roll In Story:

OCCUPATION:

Physical Description

Personality

Discerning Features

Unique Talents / Abilities:

Character TRIGGER Questions:

-Is your character considered normal and acceptable
   in this society? Why not?
- Does your character have any mannerisms, habits
   or desires considered taboo?
- What does your character do that causes others to
   feel uncomfortable?
- Does he / she have any special needs that have to
   be met (such as medication or therapy)?
- Does your character have an unknown connection
   to a famous / infamous person or group in history?
- Does your character have a deep secret that could
   change the course of events?
- What are your characters core beliefs ? Name three (3)
   principles they will not compromise.

- What is the greatest loss your character has experienced?
- What is your characters greatest fear? How does that affect
   the way they make decisions?
- What are your characters dreams? What we desire forms
   our decisions, so what does he / she want?
- Does your character have any specific prejudices? What are
   they and how do they affect interactions with others?
- Does he / she have an overpowering addiction considered a
   weakness...or perhaps a strength?
- Do they have a latent ability (or repressed memory) that
   can be brought out in the story?
- Is your character being used as a pawn in a much bigger plot
   behind the scenes?
- What lie have they told that will soon catch up & expose them?

FATHER:

FRIENDS:

MOTHER:

SIBLINGS:

HABITS / MANNERISMS

INTERNAL / EXTERNAL CONFLICTS:

PERSONAL STORY ARC

CHARACTER HISTORY

NAME _____

NICKNAME _____

BOOK _____

Series _____

IMPORTANCE				
INFLUENCE				
STRENGTH				
COORDINATION				
INTELLIGENCE				
WISDOM				
STREETWISE				
DIPLOMACY				
CHARISMA				
WILL				

Race: _____

Age: _____ Weight: _____

LAWFUL GOOD   CHAOTIC GOOD

N

LAWFUL EVIL   CHAOTIC EVIL

OCCUPATION: _____

PORTRAIT

Roll In Story:
_____
_____
_____
_____
_____
_____
_____
_____
_____
_____
_____
_____
_____

Physical Description
_____
_____
_____
_____
_____

Personality
_____
_____
_____
_____
_____
_____

Discerning Features
_____
_____
_____
_____

Unique Talents / Abilities:
_____
_____
_____
_____
_____

Character TRIGGER Questions:

- Is your character considered normal and acceptable in this society? Why not?
- Does your character have any mannerisms, habits or desires considered taboo?
- What does your character do that causes others to feel uncomfortable?
- Does he / she have any special needs that have to be met (such as medication or therapy)?
- Does your character have an unknown connection to a famous / infamous person or group in history?
- Does your character have a deep secret that could change the course of events?
- What are your characters core beliefs ? Name three (3) principles they will not compromise.

- What is the greatest loss your character has experienced?
- What is your characters greatest fear? How does that affect the way they make decisions?
- What are your characters dreams? What we desire forms our decisions, so what does he / she want?
- Does your character have any specific prejudices? What are they and how do they affect interactions with others?
- Does he / she have an overpowering addiction considered a weakness...or perhaps a strength?
- Do they have a latent ability (or repressed memory) that can be brought out in the story?
- Is your character being used as a pawn in a much bigger plot behind the scenes?
- What lie have they told that will soon catch up & expose them?

FATHER:

MOTHER:

SIBLINGS:

FRIENDS:

HABITS / MANNERISMS

INTERNAL / EXTERNAL CONFLICTS:

PERSONAL STORY ARC

CHARACTER HISTORY

NAME _____

NICKNAME _____

BOOK _____

Series _____

IMPORTANCE _____

INFLUENCE _____

STRENGTH _____

COORDINATION _____

INTELLIGENCE _____

WISDOM _____

STREETWISE _____

DIPLOMACY _____

CHARISMA _____

WILL _____

Race: _____

Age: _____

Weight: _____

PORTRAIT

LAWFUL GOOD

CHAOTIC GOOD

N

LAWFUL EVIL

CHAOTIC EVIL

OCCUPATION:

Roll In Story:

Physical Description

Personality

Discerning Features

Unique Talents / Abilities:

Character TRIGGER Questions:

-Is your character considered normal and acceptable in this society? Why not?

- Does your character have any mannerisms, habits or desires considered taboo?

- What does your character do that causes others to feel uncomfortable?

- Does he / she have any special needs that have to be met (such as medication or therapy)?

- Does your character have an unknown connection to a famous / infamous person or group in history?

- Does your character have a deep secret that could change the course of events?

- What are your characters core beliefs ? Name three (3) principles they will not compromise.

- What is the greatest loss your character has experienced?

- What is your characters greatest fear? How does that affect the way they make decisions?

- What are your characters dreams? What we desire forms our decisions, so what does he / she want?

- Does your character have any specific prejudices? What are they and how do they affect interactions with others?

- Does he / she have an overpowering addiction considered a weakness...or perhaps a strength?

- Do they have a latent ability (or repressed memory) that can be brought out in the story?

- Is your character being used as a pawn in a much bigger plot behind the scenes?

- What lie have they told that will soon catch up & expose them?

FATHER:

MOTHER:

SIBLINGS:

FRIENDS:

HABITS / MANNERISMS

INTERNAL / EXTERNAL CONFLICTS:

PERSONAL STORY ARC

CHARACTER HISTORY

NAME _____ BOOK _____

NICKNAME _____ Series _____

IMPORTANCE			
INFLUENCE			
STRENGTH			
COORDINATION			
INTELLIGENCE			
WISDOM			
STREETWISE			
DIPLOMACY			
CHARISMA			
WILL			

Race: _____

Age: _____ Weight: _____

PORTRAIT

LAWFUL
GOOD   CHAOTIC
                                      GOOD

N

LAWFUL
EVIL   CHAOTIC
                                      EVIL

OCCUPATION: _____

Roll In Story:

_____
_____
_____
_____
_____
_____
_____
_____
_____
_____
_____
_____

Physical Description

_____
_____
_____
_____
_____

Personality

_____
_____
_____
_____
_____
_____
_____

Discerning Features

_____
_____
_____
_____

Unique Talents / Abilities:

_____
_____
_____
_____

Character TRIGGER Questions:

- Is your character considered normal and acceptable in this society? Why not?
- Does your character have any mannerisms, habits or desires considered taboo?
- What does your character do that causes others to feel uncomfortable?
- Does he / she have any special needs that have to be met (such as medication or therapy)?
- Does your character have an unknown connection to a famous / infamous person or group in history?
- Does your character have a deep secret that could change the course of events?
- What are your characters core beliefs ? Name three (3) principles they will not compromise.

- What is the greatest loss your character has experienced?
- What is your characters greatest fear? How does that affect the way they make decisions?
- What are your characters dreams? What we desire forms our decisions, so what does he / she want?
- Does your character have any specific prejudices? What are they and how do they affect interactions with others?
- Does he / she have an overpowering addiction considered a weakness...or perhaps a strength?
- Do they have a latent ability (or repressed memory) that can be brought out in the story?
- Is your character being used as a pawn in a much bigger plot behind the scenes?
- What lie have they told that will soon catch up & expose them?

FATHER:

MOTHER:

SIBLINGS:

FRIENDS:

HABITS / MANNERISMS

INTERNAL / EXTERNAL CONFLICTS:

PERSONAL STORY ARC

CHARACTER HISTORY

NAME _____

NICKNAME _____

BOOK

Series

IMPORTANCE				
INFLUENCE				
STRENGTH				
COORDINATION				
INTELLIGENCE				
WISDOM				
STREETWISE				
DIPLOMACY				
CHARISMA				
WILL				

Race: _____

Age: _____   Weight: _____

LAWFUL GOOD   CHAOTIC GOOD

N

LAWFUL EVIL   CHAOTIC EVIL

OCCUPATION: _____

PORTRAIT

Roll In Story:

_____
_____
_____
_____
_____
_____
_____
_____
_____
_____
_____

Physical Description

_____
_____
_____
_____
_____

Personality

_____
_____
_____
_____
_____
_____
_____

Discerning Features

_____
_____
_____
_____
_____

Unique Talents / Abilities:

_____
_____
_____
_____
_____

Character TRIGGER Questions:

- Is your character considered normal and acceptable in this society? Why not?
- Does your character have any mannerisms, habits or desires considered taboo?
- What does your character do that causes others to feel uncomfortable?
- Does he / she have any special needs that have to be met (such as medication or therapy)?
- Does your character have an unknown connection to a famous / infamous person or group in history?
- Does your character have a deep secret that could change the course of events?
- What are your characters core beliefs? Name three (3) principles they will not compromise.

- What is the greatest loss your character has experienced?
- What is your characters greatest fear? How does that affect the way they make decisions?
- What are your characters dreams? What we desire forms our decisions, so what does he / she want?
- Does your character have any specific prejudices? What are they and how do they affect interactions with others?
- Does he / she have an overpowering addiction considered a weakness...or perhaps a strength?
- Do they have a latent ability (or repressed memory) that can be brought out in the story?
- Is your character being used as a pawn in a much bigger plot behind the scenes?
- What lie have they told that will soon catch up & expose them?

FATHER:

MOTHER:

SIBLINGS:

FRIENDS:

HABITS / MANNERISMS

INTERNAL / EXTERNAL CONFLICTS:

PERSONAL STORY ARC

CHARACTER HISTORY

NAME _____

NICKNAME _____

BOOK _____

Series _____

IMPORTANCE				
INFLUENCE				
STRENGTH				
COORDINATION				
INTELLIGENCE				
WISDOM				
STREETWISE				
DIPLOMACY				
CHARISMA				
WILL				

Race: _____

Age: _____ Weight: _____

```
LAWFUL                    CHAOTIC
GOOD                          GOOD

              N

LAWFUL                    CHAOTIC
EVIL                          EVIL
```

OCCUPATION: _____

PORTRAIT

Roll In Story:

_____
_____
_____
_____
_____
_____
_____
_____
_____
_____
_____
_____
_____

Physical Description

_____
_____
_____
_____
_____

Personality

_____
_____
_____
_____
_____

Discerning Features

_____
_____
_____
_____

Unique Talents / Abilities:

_____
_____
_____
_____

Character TRIGGER Questions:

-Is your character considered normal and acceptable in this society? Why not?

- Does your character have any mannerisms, habits or desires considered taboo?

- What does your character do that causes others to feel uncomfortable?

- Does he / she have any special needs that have to be met (such as medication or therapy)?

- Does your character have an unknown connection to a famous / infamous person or group in history?

- Does your character have a deep secret that could change the course of events?

- What are your characters core beliefs ? Name three (3) principles they will not compromise.

- What is the greatest loss your character has experienced?

- What is your characters greatest fear? How does that affect the way they make decisions?

- What are your characters dreams? What we desire forms our decisions, so what does he / she want?

- Does your character have any specific prejudices? What are they and how do they affect interactions with others?

- Does he / she have an overpowering addiction considered a weakness...or perhaps a strength?

- Do they have a latent ability (or repressed memory) that can be brought out in the story?

- Is your character being used as a pawn in a much bigger plot behind the scenes?

- What lie have they told that will soon catch up & expose them?

FATHER:

MOTHER:

SIBLINGS:

FRIENDS:

HABITS / MANNERISMS

INTERNAL / EXTERNAL CONFLICTS:

PERSONAL STORY ARC

CHARACTER HISTORY

NAME _____   **BOOK** _____

NICKNAME _____   **Series** _____

IMPORTANCE			
INFLUENCE			
STRENGTH			
COORDINATION			
INTELLIGENCE			
WISDOM			
STREETWISE			
DIPLOMACY			
CHARISMA			
WILL			

Race: _____

Age: _____   Weight: _____

PORTRAIT

LAWFUL GOOD — CHAOTIC GOOD

N

LAWFUL EVIL — CHAOTIC EVIL

OCCUPATION:

Roll In Story:
_____
_____
_____
_____
_____
_____
_____
_____
_____
_____
_____
_____
_____

Physical Description
_____
_____
_____
_____
_____

Discerning Features
_____
_____
_____
_____
_____

Personality
_____
_____
_____
_____
_____
_____
_____

Unique Talents / Abilities:
_____
_____
_____
_____

Character TRIGGER Questions:

- Is your character considered normal and acceptable in this society? Why not?
- Does your character have any mannerisms, habits or desires considered taboo?
- What does your character do that causes others to feel uncomfortable?
- Does he / she have any special needs that have to be met (such as medication or therapy)?
- Does your character have an unknown connection to a famous / infamous person or group in history?
- Does your character have a deep secret that could change the course of events?
- What are your characters core beliefs ? Name three (3) principles they will not compromise.

- What is the greatest loss your character has experienced?
- What is your characters greatest fear? How does that affect the way they make decisions?
- What are your characters dreams? What we desire forms our decisions, so what does he / she want?
- Does your character have any specific prejudices? What are they and how do they affect interactions with others?
- Does he / she have an overpowering addiction considered a weakness...or perhaps a strength?
- Do they have a latent ability (or repressed memory) that can be brought out in the story?
- Is your character being used as a pawn in a much bigger plot behind the scenes?
- What lie have they told that will soon catch up & expose them?

FATHER:

MOTHER:

SIBLINGS:

FRIENDS:

HABITS / MANNERISMS

INTERNAL / EXTERNAL CONFLICTS:

PERSONAL STORY ARC

CHARACTER HISTORY

NAME

NICKNAME

BOOK

Series

IMPORTANCE	
INFLUENCE	
STRENGTH	
COORDINATION	
INTELLIGENCE	
WISDOM	
STREETWISE	
DIPLOMACY	
CHARISMA	
WILL	

Race:

Age: **Weight:**

PORTRAIT

LAWFUL GOOD   CHAOTIC GOOD

N

LAWFUL EVIL   CHAOTIC EVIL

OCCUPATION:

Roll In Story:

Personality

Physical Description

Discerning Features

Unique Talents / Abilities:

Character TRIGGER Questions:

- Is your character considered normal and acceptable in this society? Why not?
- Does your character have any mannerisms, habits or desires considered taboo?
- What does your character do that causes others to feel uncomfortable?
- Does he / she have any special needs that have to be met (such as medication or therapy)?
- Does your character have an unknown connection to a famous / infamous person or group in history?
- Does your character have a deep secret that could change the course of events?
- What are your characters core beliefs? Name three (3) principles they will not compromise.

- What is the greatest loss your character has experienced?
- What is your characters greatest fear? How does that affect the way they make decisions?
- What are your characters dreams? What we desire forms our decisions, so what does he / she want?
- Does your character have any specific prejudices? What are they and how do they affect interactions with others?
- Does he / she have an overpowering addiction considered a weakness...or perhaps a strength?
- Do they have a latent ability (or repressed memory) that can be brought out in the story?
- Is your character being used as a pawn in a much bigger plot behind the scenes?
- What lie have they told that will soon catch up & expose them?

FATHER:

MOTHER:

SIBLINGS:

FRIENDS:

HABITS / MANNERISMS

INTERNAL / EXTERNAL CONFLICTS:

PERSONAL STORY ARC

CHARACTER HISTORY

NAME _____   BOOK _____

NICKNAME _____   Series _____

IMPORTANCE _____
INFLUENCE _____

STRENGTH _____
COORDINATION _____

INTELLIGENCE _____
WISDOM _____
STREETWISE _____
DIPLOMACY _____
CHARISMA _____
WILL _____

Race: _____

Age: _____   Weight: _____

LAWFUL   CHAOTIC
GOOD   GOOD

                N

LAWFUL   CHAOTIC
EVIL   EVIL

OCCUPATION: _____

PORTRAIT

Roll In Story:
_____
_____
_____
_____
_____
_____
_____
_____
_____
_____
_____
_____
_____
_____

Physical Description
_____
_____
_____
_____
_____
_____

Discerning Features
_____
_____
_____
_____

Personality
_____
_____
_____
_____
_____
_____
_____
_____
_____

Unique Talents / Abilities:
_____
_____
_____
_____

Character TRIGGER Questions:

-Is your character considered normal and acceptable in this society? Why not?
- Does your character have any mannerisms, habits or desires considered taboo?
- What does your character do that causes others to feel uncomfortable?
- Does he / she have any special needs that have to be met (such as medication or therapy)?
- Does your character have an unknown connection to a famous / infamous person or group in history?
- Does your character have a deep secret that could change the course of events?
- What are your characters core beliefs ? Name three (3) principles they will not compromise.

- What is the greatest loss your character has experienced?
- What is your characters greatest fear? How does that affect the way they make decisions?
- What are your characters dreams? What we desire forms our decisions, so what does he / she want?
- Does your character have any specific prejudices? What are they and how do they affect interactions with others?
- Does he / she have an overpowering addiction considered a weakness...or perhaps a strength?
- Do they have a latent ability (or repressed memory) that can be brought out in the story?
- Is your character being used as a pawn in a much bigger plot behind the scenes?
- What lie have they told that will soon catch up & expose them?

FATHER:

MOTHER:

SIBLINGS:

FRIENDS:

HABITS / MANNERISMS

INTERNAL / EXTERNAL CONFLICTS:

PERSONAL STORY ARC

CHARACTER HISTORY

NAME _____

NICKNAME _____

BOOK _____

Series _____

IMPORTANCE _____
INFLUENCE _____

STRENGTH _____
COORDINATION _____

INTELLIGENCE _____
WISDOM _____
STREETWISE _____
DIPLOMACY _____
CHARISMA _____
WILL _____

Race: _____

Age: _____   Weight: _____

LAWFUL GOOD   CHAOTIC GOOD

N

LAWFUL EVIL   CHAOTIC EVIL

OCCUPATION: _____

PORTRAIT

Roll In Story:
_____
_____
_____
_____
_____
_____
_____
_____
_____
_____
_____
_____
_____
_____
_____
_____
_____

Physical Description
_____
_____
_____
_____
_____
_____

Personality
_____
_____
_____
_____
_____
_____
_____
_____

Discerning Features
_____
_____
_____
_____

Unique Talents / Abilities:
_____
_____
_____
_____

Character TRIGGER Questions:

-Is your character considered normal and acceptable in this society? Why not?
- Does your character have any mannerisms, habits or desires considered taboo?
- What does your character do that causes others to feel uncomfortable?
- Does he / she have any special needs that have to be met (such as medication or therapy)?
- Does your character have an unknown connection to a famous / infamous person or group in history?
- Does your character have a deep secret that could change the course of events?
- What are your characters core beliefs ? Name three (3) principles they will not compromise.

- What is the greatest loss your character has experienced?
- What is your characters greatest fear? How does that affect the way they make decisions?
- What are your characters dreams? What we desire forms our decisions, so what does he / she want?
- Does your character have any specific prejudices? What are they and how do they affect interactions with others?
- Does he / she have an overpowering addiction considered a weakness...or perhaps a strength?
- Do they have a latent ability (or repressed memory) that can be brought out in the story?
- Is your character being used as a pawn in a much bigger plot behind the scenes?
- What lie have they told that will soon catch up & expose them?

FATHER:

MOTHER:

SIBLINGS:

FRIENDS:

HABITS / MANNERISMS

INTERNAL / EXTERNAL CONFLICTS:

PERSONAL STORY ARC

CHARACTER HISTORY

NAME _____

NICKNAME _____

BOOK _____

Series _____

IMPORTANCE			
INFLUENCE			
STRENGTH			
COORDINATION			
INTELLIGENCE			
WISDOM			
STREETWISE			
DIPLOMACY			
CHARISMA			
WILL			

Race: _____

Age: _____   Weight: _____

PORTRAIT

```
LAWFUL                    CHAOTIC
GOOD                        GOOD

              N

LAWFUL                    CHAOTIC
EVIL                        EVIL
```

OCCUPATION: _____

Roll In Story:

_____
_____
_____
_____
_____
_____
_____
_____
_____
_____
_____
_____
_____

Physical Description

_____
_____
_____
_____
_____
_____

Personality

_____
_____
_____
_____
_____
_____
_____
_____

Discerning Features

_____
_____
_____
_____

Unique Talents / Abilities:

_____
_____
_____
_____
_____

Character TRIGGER Questions:

-Is your character considered normal and acceptable in this society? Why not?

- Does your character have any mannerisms, habits or desires considered taboo?

- What does your character do that causes others to feel uncomfortable?

- Does he / she have any special needs that have to be met (such as medication or therapy)?

- Does your character have an unknown connection to a famous / infamous person or group in history?

- Does your character have a deep secret that could change the course of events?

- What are your characters core beliefs ? Name three (3) principles they will not compromise.

- What is the greatest loss your character has experienced?

- What is your characters greatest fear? How does that affect the way they make decisions?

- What are your characters dreams? What we desire forms our decisions, so what does he / she want?

- Does your character have any specific prejudices? What are they and how do they affect interactions with others?

- Does he / she have an overpowering addiction considered a weakness...or perhaps a strength?

- Do they have a latent ability (or repressed memory) that can be brought out in the story?

- Is your character being used as a pawn in a much bigger plot behind the scenes?

- What lie have they told that will soon catch up & expose them?

FATHER:

MOTHER:

SIBLINGS:

FRIENDS:

HABITS / MANNERISMS

INTERNAL / EXTERNAL CONFLICTS:

PERSONAL STORY ARC

CHARACTER HISTORY

NAME _____ BOOK

NICKNAME _____ Series

IMPORTANCE			
INFLUENCE			
STRENGTH			
COORDINATION			
INTELLIGENCE			
WISDOM			
STREETWISE			
DIPLOMACY			
CHARISMA			
WILL			

Race: _____

Age: _____ Weight: _____

PORTRAIT

LAWFUL GOOD   CHAOTIC GOOD

N

LAWFUL EVIL   CHAOTIC EVIL

OCCUPATION:

Roll In Story:

_____
_____
_____
_____
_____
_____
_____
_____
_____
_____
_____

Physical Description

_____
_____
_____
_____
_____

Personality

_____
_____
_____
_____
_____
_____

Discerning Features

_____
_____
_____
_____

Unique Talents / Abilities:

_____
_____
_____
_____

Character TRIGGER Questions:

- Is your character considered normal and acceptable in this society? Why not?
- Does your character have any mannerisms, habits or desires considered taboo?
- What does your character do that causes others to feel uncomfortable?
- Does he / she have any special needs that have to be met (such as medication or therapy)?
- Does your character have an unknown connection to a famous / infamous person or group in history?
- Does your character have a deep secret that could change the course of events?
- What are your characters core beliefs ? Name three (3) principles they will not compromise.

- What is the greatest loss your character has experienced?
- What is your characters greatest fear? How does that affect the way they make decisions?
- What are your characters dreams? What we desire forms our decisions, so what does he / she want?
- Does your character have any specific prejudices? What are they and how do they affect interactions with others?
- Does he / she have an overpowering addiction considered a weakness...or perhaps a strength?
- Do they have a latent ability (or repressed memory) that can be brought out in the story?
- Is your character being used as a pawn in a much bigger plot behind the scenes?
- What lie have they told that will soon catch up & expose them?

FATHER:

MOTHER:

SIBLINGS:

FRIENDS:

HABITS / MANNERISMS

INTERNAL / EXTERNAL CONFLICTS:

PERSONAL STORY ARC

CHARACTER HISTORY

NAME _____ BOOK

NICKNAME _____ Series

IMPORTANCE _____ ____ ____ ____

INFLUENCE _____ ____ ____ ____

STRENGTH _____

COORDINATION _____

INTELLIGENCE _____

WISDOM _____

STREETWISE _____

DIPLOMACY _____

CHARISMA _____

WILL _____

Race: _____

Age: _____   Weight: _____

LAWFUL   CHAOTIC
GOOD   GOOD

N

LAWFUL   CHAOTIC
EVIL   EVIL

OCCUPATION:

PORTRAIT

Roll In Story:

_____
_____
_____
_____
_____
_____
_____
_____
_____
_____
_____
_____
_____

Physical Description

_____
_____
_____
_____
_____

Personality

_____
_____
_____
_____
_____
_____
_____

Discerning Features

_____
_____
_____
_____

Unique Talents / Abilities:

_____
_____
_____
_____
_____

Character TRIGGER Questions:

- Is your character considered normal and acceptable in this society? Why not?
- Does your character have any mannerisms, habits or desires considered taboo?
- What does your character do that causes others to feel uncomfortable?
- Does he / she have any special needs that have to be met (such as medication or therapy)?
- Does your character have an unknown connection to a famous / infamous person or group in history?
- Does your character have a deep secret that could change the course of events?
- What are your characters core beliefs ? Name three (3) principles they will not compromise.

- What is the greatest loss your character has experienced?
- What is your characters greatest fear? How does that affect the way they make decisions?
- What are your characters dreams? What we desire forms our decisions, so what does he / she want?
- Does your character have any specific prejudices? What are they and how do they affect interactions with others?
- Does he / she have an overpowering addiction considered a weakness...or perhaps a strength?
- Do they have a latent ability (or repressed memory) that can be brought out in the story?
- Is your character being used as a pawn in a much bigger plot behind the scenes?
- What lie have they told that will soon catch up & expose them?

FATHER:

MOTHER:

SIBLINGS:

FRIENDS:

HABITS / MANNERISMS

INTERNAL / EXTERNAL CONFLICTS:

PERSONAL STORY ARC

CHARACTER HISTORY

NAME _____

NICKNAME _____

BOOK _____

Series _____

IMPORTANCE	
INFLUENCE	
STRENGTH	
COORDINATION	
INTELLIGENCE	
WISDOM	
STREETWISE	
DIPLOMACY	
CHARISMA	
WILL	

Race: _____

Age: _____   Weight: _____

PORTRAIT

LAWFUL GOOD		CHAOTIC GOOD
	N	
LAWFUL EVIL		CHAOTIC EVIL

OCCUPATION: _____

Roll In Story:

_____
_____
_____
_____
_____
_____
_____
_____
_____
_____
_____
_____

Physical Description

_____
_____
_____
_____
_____

Personality

_____
_____
_____
_____
_____
_____
_____

Discerning Features

_____
_____
_____
_____

Unique Talents / Abilities:

_____
_____
_____

Character TRIGGER Questions:

- Is your character considered normal and acceptable in this society? Why not?
- Does your character have any mannerisms, habits or desires considered taboo?
- What does your character do that causes others to feel uncomfortable?
- Does he / she have any special needs that have to be met (such as medication or therapy)?
- Does your character have an unknown connection to a famous / infamous person or group in history?
- Does your character have a deep secret that could change the course of events?
- What are your characters core beliefs ? Name three (3) principles they will not compromise.

- What is the greatest loss your character has experienced?
- What is your characters greatest fear? How does that affect the way they make decisions?
- What are your characters dreams? What we desire forms our decisions, so what does he / she want?
- Does your character have any specific prejudices? What are they and how do they affect interactions with others?
- Does he / she have an overpowering addiction considered a weakness...or perhaps a strength?
- Do they have a latent ability (or repressed memory) that can be brought out in the story?
- Is your character being used as a pawn in a much bigger plot behind the scenes?
- What lie have they told that will soon catch up & expose them?

FATHER:

MOTHER:

SIBLINGS:

FRIENDS:

HABITS / MANNERISMS

INTERNAL / EXTERNAL CONFLICTS:

PERSONAL STORY ARC

CHARACTER HISTORY

NAME _____ BOOK _____

NICKNAME _____ Series _____

IMPORTANCE			
INFLUENCE			
STRENGTH			
COORDINATION			
INTELLIGENCE			
WISDOM			
STREETWISE			
DIPLOMACY			
CHARISMA			
WILL			

Race: _____

Age: _____ Weight: _____

PORTRAIT

LAWFUL GOOD   CHAOTIC GOOD

N

LAWFUL EVIL   CHAOTIC EVIL

OCCUPATION:

Roll In Story:

_____
_____
_____
_____
_____
_____
_____
_____
_____
_____
_____
_____
_____
_____
_____
_____

Physical Description

_____
_____
_____
_____
_____
_____
_____

Personality

_____
_____
_____
_____
_____
_____
_____

Discerning Features

_____
_____
_____

Unique Talents / Abilities:

_____
_____
_____
_____
_____

Character TRIGGER Questions:

-Is your character considered normal and acceptable in this society? Why not?

- Does your character have any mannerisms, habits or desires considered taboo?

- What does your character do that causes others to feel uncomfortable?

- Does he / she have any special needs that have to be met (such as medication or therapy)?

- Does your character have an unknown connection to a famous / infamous person or group in history?

- Does your character have a deep secret that could change the course of events?

- What are your characters core beliefs ? Name three (3) principles they will not compromise.

- What is the greatest loss your character has experienced?

- What is your characters greatest fear? How does that affect the way they make decisions?

- What are your characters dreams? What we desire forms our decisions, so what does he / she want?

- Does your character have any specific prejudices? What are they and how do they affect interactions with others?

- Does he / she have an overpowering addiction considered a weakness...or perhaps a strength?

- Do they have a latent ability (or repressed memory) that can be brought out in the story?

- Is your character being used as a pawn in a much bigger plot behind the scenes?

- What lie have they told that will soon catch up & expose them?

FATHER:

MOTHER:

SIBLINGS:

FRIENDS:

HABITS / MANNERISMS

INTERNAL / EXTERNAL CONFLICTS:

PERSONAL STORY ARC

CHARACTER HISTORY

NAME _____   BOOK _____

NICKNAME _____   Series _____

IMPORTANCE [ ][ ][ ][ ]
INFLUENCE [ ][ ][ ][ ]

STRENGTH [ ][ ][ ][ ]
COORDINATION [ ][ ][ ][ ]

INTELLIGENCE [ ][ ][ ][ ]
WISDOM [ ][ ][ ][ ]
STREETWISE [ ][ ][ ][ ]
DIPLOMACY [ ][ ][ ][ ]
CHARISMA [ ][ ][ ][ ]
WILL [ ][ ][ ][ ]

Race:

Age: Weight:

PORTRAIT

LAWFUL GOOD   CHAOTIC GOOD

N

LAWFUL EVIL   CHAOTIC EVIL

OCCUPATION:

Roll In Story:

_____
_____
_____
_____
_____
_____
_____
_____
_____
_____
_____
_____
_____
_____

Physical Description

_____
_____
_____
_____
_____

Personality

_____
_____
_____
_____
_____
_____
_____

Discerning Features

_____
_____
_____
_____

Unique Talents / Abilities:

_____
_____
_____
_____

Character TRIGGER Questions:

-Is your character considered normal and acceptable in this society? Why not?
- Does your character have any mannerisms, habits or desires considered taboo?
- What does your character do that causes others to feel uncomfortable?
- Does he / she have any special needs that have to be met (such as medication or therapy)?
- Does your character have an unknown connection to a famous / infamous person or group in history?
- Does your character have a deep secret that could change the course of events?
- What are your characters core beliefs ? Name three (3) principles they will not compromise.

- What is the greatest loss your character has experienced?
- What is your characters greatest fear? How does that affect the way they make decisions?
- What are your characters dreams? What we desire forms our decisions, so what does he / she want?
- Does your character have any specific prejudices? What are they and how do they affect interactions with others?
- Does he / she have an overpowering addiction considered a weakness...or perhaps a strength?
- Do they have a latent ability (or repressed memory) that can be brought out in the story?
- Is your character being used as a pawn in a much bigger plot behind the scenes?
- What lie have they told that will soon catch up & expose them?

FATHER:

MOTHER:

SIBLINGS:

FRIENDS:

HABITS / MANNERISMS

INTERNAL / EXTERNAL CONFLICTS:

PERSONAL STORY ARC

CHARACTER HISTORY

NAME

NICKNAME

BOOK

Series

IMPORTANCE				
INFLUENCE				
STRENGTH				
COORDINATION				
INTELLIGENCE				
WISDOM				
STREETWISE				
DIPLOMACY				
CHARISMA				
WILL				

Race:

Age:

Weight:

PORTRAIT

LAWFUL GOOD

CHAOTIC GOOD

N

LAWFUL EVIL

CHAOTIC EVIL

OCCUPATION:

Roll In Story:

Physical Description

Personality

Discerning Features

Unique Talents / Abilities:

Character TRIGGER Questions:

- Is your character considered normal and acceptable in this society? Why not?
- Does your character have any mannerisms, habits or desires considered taboo?
- What does your character do that causes others to feel uncomfortable?
- Does he / she have any special needs that have to be met (such as medication or therapy)?
- Does your character have an unknown connection to a famous / infamous person or group in history?
- Does your character have a deep secret that could change the course of events?
- What are your characters core beliefs? Name three (3) principles they will not compromise.

- What is the greatest loss your character has experienced?
- What is your characters greatest fear? How does that affect the way they make decisions?
- What are your characters dreams? What we desire forms our decisions, so what does he / she want?
- Does your character have any specific prejudices? What are they and how do they affect interactions with others?
- Does he / she have an overpowering addiction considered a weakness…or perhaps a strength?
- Do they have a latent ability (or repressed memory) that can be brought out in the story?
- Is your character being used as a pawn in a much bigger plot behind the scenes?
- What lie have they told that will soon catch up & expose them?

FATHER:

MOTHER:

SIBLINGS:

FRIENDS:

HABITS / MANNERISMS

INTERNAL / EXTERNAL CONFLICTS:

PERSONAL STORY ARC

CHARACTER HISTORY

Subject:

Subject:

Subject:

Subject:

© 2015 Jaime D. Buckley INC. Find more advanced writing tools at AdvancedWorldbuilding.com

Subject:

Subject:

Subject:

Subject:

Subject:

Subject:

Subject:

Subject:

Subject:

Subject:

Subject:

Subject:

Subject:

Subject:

Subject:

Subject:

Subject:

Subject:

Subject:

Subject:

Subject:

Subject:

Subject:

Subject:

Subject:

Subject:

Subject:

Subject:

Subject:

Subject:

Subject:

Subject:

Subject:

Subject:

Subject:

Subject:

Subject:

Subject:

Subject:

Subject:

Subject:

Subject:

Subject:

Subject:

Subject:

Subject:

Subject:

Subject:

Subject:

Subject:

Subject:

Subject:

Subject:

Subject:

Subject:

Subject:

Subject:

Subject:

Subject:

Subject:

Subject:

Subject:

Subject:

Subject:

Subject:

WORLDBUILDING INDEX

TOPIC	PAGES

WORLDBUILDING INDEX

TOPIC   PAGES

WORLDBUILDING INDEX

TOPIC	PAGES

WORLDBUILDING INDEX

TOPIC	PAGES

WORLDBUILDING INDEX

TOPIC	PAGES

WORLDBUILDING INDEX

TOPIC	PAGES

WORLDBUILDING INDEX

TOPIC   PAGES

WORLDBUILDING INDEX

TOPIC	PAGES

WORLDBUILDING INDEX

TOPIC   PAGES

About the Author

JAIME BUCKLEY IS A husband, father of 12, grandfather, author, professional illustrator & popular parenting blogger. When he's not engaged in hunting monsters, acting as a survival flotation device or a master sliver-picker-outer (just ask his little kids), he's also a cartoonist, game creator, podcaster and avid teacher.

Jaime is best known for his **Chronicles of a Hero** series and his book **Advanced WORLDBUILDING**, a guide to assist writers in building fictional worlds faster, easier and in more detail than ever before.

He lives in Utah with his wife, Kathilynn, his organically grown fan club and loves communicating with readers all over the world. You can connect with Jaime through his various websites.

If the mood strikes you, email him at jaimebuckley@wantedhero.com (he'll be so excited).

It might take him a while, but he always emails back.

Other Books by
Jaime Buckley

Chronicles of a Hero

Hobin Luckyfeller's Fieldguide

WHAT IF
(choose-your-own-ending)

Short Stories

Wordbuilding

Watch for our new series
WORLDBUILDING INC

See the full (and growing) list of books at:
http://wantedhero.com/all-books

Made in the USA
Las Vegas, NV
16 December 2021

38163211R00219